GERMAN DIARY

GERMAN DIARY

by

FENNER BROCKWAY

LONDON
VICTOR GOLLANCZ LTD
1946

PRINTED IN GREAT BRITAIN BY RICHARD CLAY AND COMPANY, LTD.
BUNGAY, SUFFOLK.

I WOULD like to dedicate this book to four people : *Fred Perkins*, an English soldier in Hamburg who inspired my visit to Germany, *Kurt Schumacher*, the leader of the reborn Socialist Movement in Germany, *Heinz Heydorn*, one of the leaders of the new Socialist Youth of Germany, and *Major Luxton*, an officer of the Occupation for whom freedom has no frontiers.

AUTHOR'S PREFACE

SINCE THIS Diary was written, the position in the British zone in Germany has deteriorated seriously. This is clear from the reports of all observers and is confirmed by the letters which I am receiving from both British personnel and Germans. "Things are getting steadily worse," writes a British official. "There is no doubt that there is a rising feeling against the British," writes a soldier. "The enthusiasm for the English is disappearing everywhere," writes a prominent German Trade Unionist. "Only Nazis and militarists are satisfied: the Occupation is fulfilling their prophecies. The people are either looking towards Russia, reverting to Nazism or finding an escape in Nihilism."

Let us acknowledge the advances carried through since these pages were written. The economy of the British and American zones has been co-ordinated. A part of the German fishing fleet has been restored. The steel industry of the Ruhr has been taken over with a view to nationalisation. An amnesty has been granted to Nazis under twenty-seven years of age on the ground that they never had an opportunity to acquire any other political faith. Rations have been increased by 200 calories a day.

But these measures are woefully inadequate compared with the general deterioration which has set in. Why this worsening? "It is mainly due," writes the soldier whom I have already quoted, "to the continuing food shortage, the eviction of Germans from their homes, and the feeling of frustration at the absence of any plan to reorganise production in the British zone."

Take these points in turn. The basic ration in the towns of the British zone has been increased, but it is *still less than half* of ours at home. The cases of Hunger-Oedema and tuberculosis in the hospitals continue to mount. (See Appendix.) The discontent with the food shortage is increased by the reports which are received from the Russian zone that rations have been increased there—and by the daily contrast with the standard of life which the British personnel are enjoying in the midst of the German hunger.

The seizure of German homes and furniture to serve British staff needs and to house their families has caused a wave of resentment more bitter than any since the Occupation. In Hamburg, where thousands are already living in cellars and shelters, thirty thousand people* have been turned into the streets and a large part of their furniture confiscated. This mass eviction is not primarily for the purpose of accommodating the wives and children of British personnel, but for the provision of new British headquarters for the zone. It is natural that the people should be bitter when housing materials and workmen are utilised on this elaborate "Hamburg Project".

The third ground for despair among the German people is the lack of evidence of any plan for industrial reorganisation and recovery in the British zone. The British have recently called in the services of Dr. Agartz, the Socialist economic expert, but so far the German people have to bear their present privations without any ground to hope for better things in the future. They see no end to the tunnel of inhuman existence in which they grope darkly. There is no sign of a constructive plan to enable them to cling to the light.

Here again they are observing the difference in the Russian zone, where industrial reorganisation is proceeding rapidly. Their memories of the early Russian ruthlessness in dismantling workplaces and homes become dim as they hear of the busy factories and the developing production which is now proceeding. The higher rations in the Russian zone may be an election bribe, the busy factories may be serving the Russian economy rather than a planned Germany economy; but hungry and destitute people don't pause to weigh these political and long-term considerations. They see recovery being organised in the Russian zone whilst in the British zone industry remains stagnant—and their hopes begin to turn to Russia.

An as international Socialist, I am not concerned whether Russia or Britain is the instrument which provides food and industrial recovery to Germany. I want the hunger to be ended, I want the German people to have the opportunity to lift themselves from Nazism and War and their consequences, and to become a partner in a co-operative world. I want that

* This is the official estimate. German Socialists say that it is based on the normal population of the two affected districts and overlooks the overcrowding which followed bomb destruction. They estimate the number of evicted people at 80,000.

as a matter of human decency and freedom apart from any political considerations. But I am also a Democratic Socialist and I want the future Germany to be a Democratic Socialist, rather than a Totalitarian Communist, State. I love liberty, and no democrat who has learned of Russian methods in Germany, as I did during my visit, would wish to see them extended.

Germany is now the battleground on which the issue of Democratic Socialism or Totalitarian Communism for the whole of Europe may be decided. Many of those serving in the Political Section of the British administration in Germany understand this. I think Mr. John Hynd understands it. But at present this understanding is being only timidly reflected in policy. The British are giving a certain degree of support to the Social Democrats as against the Communists; but because of the growing unpopularity of the British this may prove to be a handicap to the Social Democrats rather than a help. The way to help Democratic Socialism in Germany is to provide the conditions and the opportunity for it to function.

We have a Labour Government. It should be the leadership of Democratic Socialism in Germany, Europe and the world. Believing that a Democratic Socialist Germany is the surest guarantee that Nazism will not revive and that Germany will grow to co-operate with other peoples to maintain peace, realising that what happens in Germany will be perhaps the biggest factor in determining the future pattern of Europe, our Government should consciously plan to create conditions in the British zone which are a model of the Democratic Socialist approach.

In the final pages of this book I have outlined a suggested Socialist policy for Germany. I repeat that I am aware of the difficulties—the difficulty of the world food shortage, the difficulty of planning industrial recovery in the British zone whilst there is the shortage of Ruhr coal. But no one can be blind to the unequal distribution of food in the world, to the contrast between the hunger in Germany and the plenty just across its frontiers, some of which could reach Germany if its industries were restarted so that goods were available for export in exchange. Nor can one accept the view that nothing can be done on a big scale to restart those industries until more Ruhr coal is available. So long as we are responsible for the administration of the British zone, we should plan its industrial recovery with no less thoroughness than we should apply if the territory were British, and we should utilise all world resources to get its industries going. At present German industry is treated as a Cinderella, at the end of the queue. Germans have some reason for suspecting that we are more concerned to extort the secrets of their industrial processes for the benefit of British capitalist enterprises than to get their factories at work again.

Britain can make this new approach to the German problem, but even so it would not be solved. Unless relations between Britain, America and Russia are improved, Germany will remain divided, her nationhood denied, and the frontier between its Western and Eastern zones will become the frontier of the Third World War. This leads to a question which goes beyond the scope of this book, but I believe the answer is to be found in the extension of the policy which I have urged for Germany—in the adoption of a challengingly Socialist policy, democratic and international, in all foreign affairs. British policy towards Indonesia, Greece, Spain, to cite only three examples, gives Russia reason for concluding that there has been no change, that there is a continuity with the Tory imperialist policy which preceded it. We need, not only in Germany but everywhere in the world, a foreign policy which breaks completely with Britain's imperialist past, which boldly gives a lead to the peoples to turn to a Democratic Socialism which is internationally inspired. If that became our policy, openly avowed and courageously practised, Russia would have no ground for maintaining her doubts, and her power to misinterpret our aims and actions to the millions of people under her influence would progressively diminish.

Britain should be as clearly the instrument of Democratic Socialism in the world as Russia is the instrument of Totalitarian Communism. When we become that, millions of the common peoples of all lands will rally to us as allies and we shall be in a position to reach an understanding with Russia, accepting the economic basis of Socialism which is hers, but determined to maintain in Britain, and wherever our influence extends, the superstructure of democracy and liberty which is particularly ours.

Without such an agreement, there is no hope of Germany becoming a political and economic unit, a united democratic nation in a peaceful world.

FENNER BROCKWAY.

September, 1946.

P.S.—As these pages went to press, news came of the American "New Deal" for Germany. It defined the future

x

function of the Allies as "control and inspection" and declared for a democratic government through a constituent assembly for the whole of Germany and a national council representative of state and provincial governments. It declared that the time had come to settle peace terms with a German government and re-opened the question of the extent of the territory to be ceded to Poland on the east. It insisted that Germany should be an economic unit and that industry should be levelled upwards if reparations are to be taken from current output.

Simultaneously it was announced that German executives are to be set up for the joint control of economic affairs in the American and British zones. They will control food rationing, distribution of food imports, taxation, customs, and production for foreign trade.

This is a welcome advance and, if Russia and France will support these proposals, new hope will come to Germany. But if democracy is to have a chance, Germany must get the foodstuffs she needs to conquer hunger and the raw materials she needs to restart housing and industry: *without these, elaborate schemes for democratic constitutions will count for little*. Given the opportunity, Germany may yet become not only a successful democracy, but a Democratic Socialist society.

Will Russia concur? By the time this is read, events may have given the answer. I hope for the sake of Europe it is favourable.

THE FIRST DAY

April 28th, 1946.

BRITISH DEMOCRACY is a strange thing. Here am I, a critic
of the war, a critic of the Potsdam Agreement, in many respects
a critic of the Labour Government, and I am going to Germany with all the facilities which the British army and the
British Government can provide !

It was surprisingly easy, no red-tape, no delay. I write to
the Ministry of Information and by return an official replies
saying I can go if my application as a newspaper man is endorsed by the Newspaper and Periodical Emergency Council.
I write to the NPEC and the Chairman replies that he has
forwarded endorsement to the War Office. I 'phone the War
Office and make an appointment for that afternoon.

Then my first surprise. The War Office annexe, to which I
am directed, is opposite Downing Street; it is a small square
building like a concrete fort. I descend steps—and find myself
in an underworld of concrete and steel, passages foreshorten-
ing into the distance, criss-crossing, numbered offices lining
them. I walk for ten minutes and am lost utterly. I enquire
the way from a soldier, walk another ten minutes and once
more face the soldier.

"What, you here again?" he exclaims and decides to guide
me.

I am shown into an office where a uniformed young woman
sits at a neatly arranged table. She is the Public Relations
Officer. She takes forms from a drawer, asks questions with
friendly efficiency, fills in the particulars. It is all very simple.
I ask whether I can reach the earth's surface in any more
direct way.

"Certainly. Turn to the left and you will find an exit near
the National Liberal Club."

Only Londoners will appreciate the significance of this
reply. The National Liberal Club must be a quarter of a mile
from Downing Street. Unknown to the thousands who daily
walk Whitehall, all this area is honeycombed with underground offices, a carefully-kept secret of the war. I suppose
it was in the bowels of the earth here that Mr. Churchill and

1

his Cabinet colleagues transacted their business during the blitz.

I had got my papers. All I wanted was my "War Correspondent's" uniform. Why War Correspondent? Why a uniform? It was explained to me that the Peace Treaty was not signed and that correspondents could enjoy facilities in Germany only if they wore uniform. Would I be allowed to go where I liked, see whom I liked, write what I liked? Of course, unless circumstances became abnormal. O.K.—I would take the uniform. But I smiled as I collected it at Chelsea Barracks, remembering that in 1919 my disciplinary record had been so bad that I was warned I would be liable to two years' hard labour if I should ever seek to become associated with the Forces again!

This ready permission to visit Germany as a journalist was a surprise, but a bigger surprise followed. I had sent word to Hamburg that I hoped to come, with the result that I had an invitation from the Trades Council to speak at their May Day demonstration. I was thrilled at the prospect, but I didn't think it would come off. To write in the British press about Germany was one thing, to speak at a German public meeting another; but doubtfully I decided to ask permission, writing to both Mr. Bevin and Mr. Hynd. Permission came. When I read Mr. Hynd's letter my appreciation of the tolerance of British democracy rose with a bound. I doubt whether there is another country in the world which would have allowed it.

Even now this toleration had not reached its limits. A German Socialist friend, a refugee from Nazism since the early thirties, asked me whether there was any means by which he could accompany me. Well, it would make a good journalistic story—a Socialist returning to Germany after ten years' exclusion and writing his impression of the change. I contacted Emrys Hughes, M.P., editor of the Scottish Socialist weekly, *Forward*. He saw the possibilities of the story—and within three days Wolf Nelki had got his papers and his uniform. He is travelling overland to-day whilst I go by air. We shall meet at Hamburg.

BY AIR TO HAMBURG

London is teeming with rain this Sunday morning as I make my way to the R.A.F. booking office in St. James's Street. There is a lounge with comfortable seats where we await the bus for Croydon. Eighteen of us mount the bus—a typical army major, a more approachable American officer, an

UNRRA official, fourteen N.C.O.s and privates. We are unusually silent, even for Britishers. When a young R.A.F. girl suddenly exclaims, "How I wish I weren't going back!" everyone is startled, but perhaps her cry is the explanation of the silence. All are returning from leave.

At the aerodrome we exchange money into marks, are given a look-over by the Security people, and are served sandwiches and cups of tea in a lounge. I am puzzled about money. I am allowed £5 in sterling and £5 in marks. How can I travel from Hamburg to Berlin, from Berlin to the Ruhr, from the Ruhr to Hanover and back to Hamburg on that? How can I live in addition? I wonder, but I don't worry: I shall find out.

My encounter with the Security officials is amusing. There is the very same officer whom I met in 1937 when I was last at Croydon—the officer who, on instructions, turned back three of my Spanish Socialist friends who intended to speak at meetings in this country against Franco. How the wheel has turned in the intervening nine years (though not yet completely)! He recognises me and smiles enigmatically.

The plane is an American Dakota troop-carrier, with comfortable seats but no other amenities, except luncheon boxes. The rounded green roof is covered with gadgets, tubes and oxygen containers. We see nothing of England, flying above brownish clouds, but over the North Sea the clouds thin, and by the time we reach Holland and Germany the sun has conquered. Great tracts of the earth in Holland are still flooded. Germany is a beautiful quilt of green fields and little red towns, with no marks of war until we reach the suburbs of Hamburg. Then vast areas of destruction.

A SOCIALIST WELCOME

On a board in the reception-room at the aerodrome is a notice saying a car is waiting for me. A British soldier friend approaches—and with him is Karl Meitmann, Social Democratic leader at Hamburg, and his twenty-three-year-old daughter. I haven't seen Karl since 1931. His hair is now silver, but he is bubbling with enthusiasm and friendliness, as he was then. "You are the first Socialist from another country to come to us," he says with emotion. In the car I somewhat diffidently hand to Grete, his daughter, a sausage roll and cake which I had not eaten in the plane. There is no artificial restraint in her acceptance. "Oh, mother will be glad of them," she exclaims. This is my introduction to the food problem. I see a woman scratching in the earth at the edge of

3

the concrete road. "What is she looking for?" I ask. "Coal—or anything to burn," replies Grete. My introduction to the fuel problem.

We pull up at the Esplanade Hotel, the headquarters of the British Military Government, but it is Sunday afternoon and the offices are deserted. On the advice of my soldier friend I go to the Officers' Transit Mess at Streit's Hotel and am booked in by a young Jewish sergeant. In England we should call this hotel Victorian—heavy decorations and upholstered chairs—but it is more than comfortable. In my room are two wooden bedsteads and an army iron bedstead. A Mil. Gov. official (the abbreviation which everyone uses) is tidying up before dinner. He is a Scot of Scots. "I hope we're alone to-night," he says. "Last night I shared with two lively young R.A.F. boys. At one o'clock they tried to think up an excuse to summon the chambermaid, and decided on hot-water bottles. Whish, was she angry? For once I was on the German side." He notices my pipe. "And they filled the room with smoke," he adds.

My First Meal in Germany

I go down to the restaurant for my first meal in Germany. I know of the hunger and wonder what it will be. An orchestra of rather weedy men is playing in the lounge as I pass through. The restaurant is bright, the ornate walls repainted, shining cutlery is on the tables. Service officers and Mil. Gov. officials, men and women, all in uniform, sit in twos and fours; waiters in boiled shirts move among them. How absurdly English these waiters look—far more English than most staffs in London restaurants!

My waiter asks for my ticket. Ticket? Yes, they can be had at the reception office. I enquire of the sergeant there and he gives me three—breakfast, luncheon and dinner. How much? One mark—sixpence for a day's board! I'm beginning to see why I don't need much money. I return to the restaurant and look at the menu: *Minestra—Jambon de Virginie glacee au Burgundy, Petits pois au Beurre, Pommes Croquettes—Coup Maison—Fromage—Cafe.** Soup, Ham dressed with Burgundy, Peas in butter, Potato Croquets, Ice Cream, Cheese, Coffee. Not bad

* The fare at this Transit Hotel proves typical of the meals provided for officers in Germany, so I will quote also the menus for breakfast and lunch. *Breakfast:* Stewed Fruit, Porridge with Milk—Buttered Egg and Diced Bacon—Tea, Bread, Butter—Preserves. *Luncheon:* Windsor Soup—Boiled Brisket of Beef, Mustard Sauce, Dressed Cabbage, Parmentier Potatoes—Albemarle Puddling, Cream Sauce—Tea.

for a starving country. I tell the waiter I am a vegetarian. "Certainly, sir," he says in perfect English. "Perhaps an omelette?" Each course is generous and well-cooked: the omelette stretches from edge to edge of the plate, two fresh eggs must have gone to its making. I calculate my meal at over 1,200 calories, feel more than a little ashamed as I remember that nine million Germans* are on a *daily* ration of 1,000 calories.

My coffee drunk and my pipe lighted, I prepare to sit in the lounge to listen to the music, but my soldier friend arrives to take me to Karl Meitmann's flat. Outside the hotel is Karl himself with his car—I learn that as Social Democratic chairman he is allowed a car and petrol, a privilege extended also to leaders of the two rival parties, the Communist Party and the Christian Democratic Union. We drive to a district of large houses, fronted with gardens. It reminds me of Hampstead. I remark that the bomb damage does not seem more serious than London. "You wait," says my soldier friend, grimly. As in Hampstead, the houses have been divided into flats. Karl's is on the third floor.

In a German Socialist's Home

I am shown into a crowded little sitting-room. Round a low table, occupying easy-chairs and a settee, is a mixed group: Germans and Allies in uniform. We are welcomed by Karl's wife, a little, cheerful woman, their daughter Grete, and her brother, perhaps two years younger. I recognise a Mil. Gov. official—I had known him first twenty years ago as a member of the Youth Section of the I.L.P. of Holland and more recently as a Left Socialist in London. He is now in charge of one of the most important industries in Hamburg. He introduces me to a colleague in uniform, a Dutch official, also a Socialist. There is a fair young German, whom I like immediately—tall and slight, his cheeks pinched, thoughtful, friendly and—am I right?—with a memory of suffering in his eyes. We drink black tea and are soon talking and laughing like old friends—this group from three nations which, but a year ago, were at war. All speak fluently in English, except Frau Meitmann, to whom Grete translates the tit-bits in occasional whispers.

Our talk begins inevitably with Karl's memories of our last meeting. It was at the International Socialist Conference at Vienna, two years before Hitler's victory. "I can still see James Maxton on that platform," says Karl, "his long black

* This is the number on the lowest rations in the British zone.

5

hair, his pointing finger. I can still hear his warning to us, uttered in that deep, grave voice, the warning that if we relied for help on the bankers of London, Paris and New York our cause was lost. How right he was!" I tell him that Maxton is seriously ill. "Oh dear, how sad!—I must write to him, our Party must write to him. You shall take the letter back. He is the soul of International Socialism." *

I ask questions to get a kind of overall picture before I set out on my investigations. Is there really hunger? Both Englishmen and Germans round the table smile sardonically. Every German, they tell me, is hungry—except a handful who are the core of the black market. A great many Germans are starving. Is the black market extensive? Of course; when you can't get enough on the legal ration all of you get food illegally if you can. How? By exchanging valuable articles with those who somehow have got a store of food, or with shopkeepers; by going into the country at week-ends and trading with farmers— but very often the police search your parcels at the station or the sack on the back of your bicycle, and your precious store is confiscated. What proportion of the population gets more than the ration in these ways? Who knows? Off and on, a considerable proportion. If they didn't, they'd be falling in the streets.

But remember this, says the fair young German with emphasis, there are a lot of folk, the most helpless, those who always are the first victims when things are short, the old folk, spinsters getting on in life, single persons who have to depend on themselves, the lame and disabled, those who are not so bright mentally—these people, and they add up to thousands, *never* get more than the 1,000 calorie-ration, and they are starving day by day.

What are the people thinking? Karl answers. When the British entered Hamburg, they were welcomed by a very large part of the population, especially the working-class, as liberators. Hamburg had always been a Socialist and Communist stronghold; it had never gone so pro-Nazi as most parts of Germany. This friendly attitude towards the British continued until the end of the year despite the lack of fuel, but since January there has been a sharp and increasing change. This is mostly due to the food situation. It isn't much good lecturing hungry people on the world shortage, especially when they see the British officials living so well and when they know

* These letters reached Maxton shortly before his death and cheered him greatly.

6

that in Belgium and Denmark food stocks are plentiful. More and more of the people are beginning to say "it wasn't so bad under the Nazis" or "it isn't so bad in the Russian zone" (note: *Is* it? I must check up on this).

Two other things are adding to a growth of anti-British feeling, Karl says. The first is the way in which housing accommodation has been commandeered for the British personnel and German families turned out. There is a rumour that a large quarter of the city is to be taken over for permanent headquarters for the British occupying forces and that big-scale building is to be done for them. This is causing indignation, because thousands of people in the city, bombed out of their homes, are still existing in the shelters. (I can see this becoming serious.)*

The other thing which is causing dismay is the slowness of industrial recovery and the prospect that, under the Potsdam Agreement, Hamburg's huge shipbuilding works will be dismantled. "We never want to see another battleship or submarine built here," exclaims Karl emphatically. "We are prepared for every kind of inspection to prevent it. But why shouldn't our workmen, who are so skilled at the job, why shouldn't our shipyards, which are so well adapted for the job, be used to make ships for trade and commerce? Let them make ships for other countries, if you like; but why—why waste this for all the world?"

I enquire about the revival of the Trade Union and Socialist Movement. The Germans smile proudly. "You shall see on May Day," Grete promises. They hurl figures at me. Trade Unionists—134,000. Social Democrats—24,000. Communists —14,000.

A Socialist Youth Leader

Karl motors me back to Streit's Hotel and my soldier friend to his billet. I ask about the fair young German who has attracted me. Hs is Heinz Joachim Heydorn, leader of the Socialist Youth in Hamburg. What is his story? The reply surprises me. In August, 1939, he was German master at Rydal School in North Wales. He deliberately returned to Germany because he believed that war would inevitably bring the social revolution. Disillusioned, he deserted from the German army after a year and successfully carried on in the illegal under-

* In July women demonstrated angrily against further evictions and four political parties—Social Democrats, Communists, Christian Democrats and Free Democrats—held a joint meeting of protest.

ground movement until he learned that the Gestapo were on his track. Then he escaped into France and was finally made a prisoner by the British. It was a shock to him that he should be held as a prisoner at all, but at length his anti-Nazi record won him liberation. He returned at once to Hamburg to help win the youth, and especially the students, for Socialism. "He is the most promising comrade we have of the new generation," says Karl.

My Scottish companion is under the sheets and asleep when I enter the bedroom. There are no R.A.F. boys to disturb us. I refrain from taking my usual goodnight smoke.

THE SECOND DAY

April 29th, 1946.

I WAS told in London that my address here would be 5 P.R.S. It occurs to me that it is about time I found it. After breakfast I go to a 'phone box, and within a few seconds I am through. "Brockway? Oh yes, we expected you last night. Where did you stay? Streit's? Oh, we'll do better for you than that. We've a very cosy little War Correspondents' Mess here. Come straight along and we'll fix you up." I offer to pay for the 'phone call. "Pay!" exclaims the sergeant. "Mil. Gov. never pays." I ask for a bill for my room and bed. "Nothing," he remarks. "Mil. Gov. pays everything."

The headquarters of 5 P.R.S. are at the near-end of the second lake, Alster Lake. I decide to walk. It's a beautiful day, blue sky and sunshine. I discover that Hamburg is also beautiful, at least the Hamburg I am in here. I cross the road and am on the bank of the first lake, with white-sailed yachts corvetting on its surface. Round three sides are hotels, offices, large houses, fronted by tree-lined boulevards. Away in the distance, on the farther side, there seems to be an embankment carrying an unobtrusive railway. I am reminded of Stockholm. There is little evidence of bombing, except at one corner.

As I walk I look at the people. The first glance brings a surprise: they are well-dressed—better, I think, than at home. Then I look again, and notice the frequency of ill-looking faces, grey and yellow, lines running from eyes to mouth, protruding cheek-bones. These are mostly the older people, but not only. . . . I cannot look at them—and then my eyes seek them out again. I begin to count. They are about one in five. Never anywhere else have I seen these gaunt features passing with such regularity. I stand against a kiosk and watch. I find myself shrinking from this examination. Why? One stands on the edge of a passing stream of people in London and there is no restraint in one's interest and curiosity. I notice another thing. The absence of colour. There is no freshness in their cheeks, no brown or tinge of red. A dull greyness, or that more dreadful yellow. Last night I asked about hunger. Good God, there is no need to ask! It is evident to anyone with eyes.

I turn at the foot of the lake and walk along the roadway at its side. I don't look into the faces of the people. I am ashamed. I wonder what they are thinking, thinking of the well-fed, uniformed Englishmen who walk their streets.

Then I pass an English Tommy walking arm in arm with a girl. That makes me look into faces again, to see if there is any resentment. No, not a sign of it: the soldier and his German girl are accepted as quite ordinary.

What *are* these people thinking, these people who have gone through the war as we have, but who have known Nazism and its defeat, who have had its beastliness exposed to themselves and the world, who now have to accept an army of occupation and an alien government? What are they thinking of us? I try to imagine how I would feel if the German army were in occupation in London.

This time I look into their eyes openly, from one to another as they pass. Most of them meet my glance without expression, neither friendliness nor enmity. Now and again a woman smiles invitingly, or a man responds with a look of half greeting, occasionally there is curt antagonism, but most turn their eyes away without any sign of feeling.

I was told last night that many of these folk welcomed the British army as liberators; they certainly don't look at me now as though I were a liberator. My main impression is of neutrality, indecision, almost a vacuum. I ponder on it. A vacuum cannot last. How will it be filled?

WHERE JOURNALISTS STAY

I reach the end of the lake, pass under a railway bridge—and face a still larger and more beautiful lake. Except for a short row of nearby buildings, we have got away from offices and shops. This is obviously where the rich of Hamburg live (or lived). Houses stand in their own grounds, the road is broad and lined with large trees on either side, between the road and the lake is a track for horse-riding and then grass down to the water's edge.

One of the few shops is labelled "5 P.R.S." A soldier takes me to an inner office, where a friendly captain offers to help me in any way I want, including the service of a car. "The first thing," he said, "is to get settled in at Warcormess." I look puzzled. "The War Correspondents' mess," he explains. I take a car immediately, collecting my bag from Streit's *en route*. Warcormess had been a private house of a wealthy Nazi. It stands back in a well-kept garden, a beautiful group of trees shading a smooth, deep green lawn. I'm welcomed by a young German woman, dark and all smiles. My room overlooks the garden at the back, flower-beds, a rustic seat under a copper beech, blossoming fruit trees in the distance. There are twin beds : I ask that the second shall be reserved for my friend, Wolf, who ought to be here this evening. Leaving, I stand at the foot of the steps a moment and feast my eyes on the view across the lake, through the trees, rich in spring colouring, which rise from the grassy border on the farther side of the road. The wealthy Nazis knew where to live—and so does the Mil. Gov.

I whirl back along the bank of the lake to 5 P.R.S. and am back with the friendly officer again. When he hears that I'm interested in politics, he 'phones the Political Officer of Mil. Gov., who asks me to go and see him at once at the Esplanade.

HAMBURG'S POLITICAL OFFICER

The Political Officer is a Major Luxton, a young man of about thirty, wearing the uniform of the Parachute Regiment. He welcomes me as a fellow Socialist and summons four other officers to meet me. I don't know who they all are, but recognise the Industrial Relations Officer, Mr. Sherwood, who used to be secretary to Will Thorne, M.P., and was on Margaret Bondfield's staff when she was Minister of Labour. "I'm afraid I gave you some trouble in those days," I remark, remembering the conflict which our group of "rebel M.P.s" had with his chief over unemployment benefits. He laughs. When the others go, Sherwood remains behind to tell me about the rebirth of the Trade Union Movement, his main sphere of activity and one about which he is evidently enthusiastic. It is certainly something to be pleased about.

THE REBORN TRADE UNION MOVEMENT

At this point I am in a difficulty. One of the officers who has just gone out was the Public Relations Officer. He told me that there is absolutely no censorship on what I write about Germany but there is one rule which correspondents are asked to accept. No official of Mil. Gov. must be quoted by name. Well, that seemed reasonable when he said it; but it will be confoundedly awkward in writing this diary. I must not quote Mr. Sherwood : here, nevertheless, is the story of the reborn Trade Union Movement in Hamburg. Accept the facts as from, not Mr. Sherwood, but the Mil. Gov. as a whole. Accept the comments as from me only.

A year ago there was not a single free Trade Union in Hamburg. Now there are thirteen, with a membership of 130,475 (the return for a month ago). This high figure, which represents one-fourth of the working population of the city, has been achieved "without any propaganda or recruitment drive other than that carried out by individual members." Great difficulties have had to be overcome. It has been difficult, for example, to find meeting-places in many parts of Hamburg because of the bomb destruction. When they have been found, there has been no heating during the winter months. When the only available meeting-places have been at some distance, there has been little or no transport. It says a great deal for the enthusiasm of the builders of the re-created Trade Union Movement that they should not have been deterred by these obstacles. It says still more, perhaps, for the instinctive support of the *idea* of Trade Unionism that such a big movement should have been built up within a year.

Let us pause for a moment and consider. For twelve years there were no free Trades Unions in Germany. Many of the leaders and officials of the old movement were taken away to prisons and concentration camps; many died. Yet the spirit of Trade Unionism has proved to be so unconquerable that, as soon as organisation was again possible, there were men to be found in the factories, the docks, the railway yards who were prepared to devote themselves, regardless of difficulties, to its reconstruction, and there were more than one hundred thousand workers who were ready to follow their lead. That strikes me as a mighty fact, showing that working-class solidarity and self-reliance have lived despite all the domination and terror of Nazism.

How have the new Unions been formed? Mil. Gov. insists that they are spontaneous and autonomous: they are not promoted from above. First comes the expression of a desire by a body of workers to form a Union: then the Industrial Relations Section of Mil. Gov. co-operates with guidance.

The embryonic Unions pass through three stages. *Phase I.*— Groups of workers meet to discuss the proposal to form a Union and elect representatives to prepare plans of organisation. *Phase II.*—The organisation proceeds on the basis of these plans. Members are recruited and a constitution is drawn up for their approval. *Phase III.*—The "established" stage, when the members have approved the constitution and have elected their officials according to it. In Hamburg such progress has been made that the thirteen Unions are in the final stage of Phase II and will shortly reach Phase III.

I am interested to learn the basis of organisation because the Trade Union Movement everywhere is divided on this issue.

In America the struggle between the industrial Unions, representing *all* workers in an industry, and the craft Unions, representing particular occupations which sometimes cross the frontiers of industries, has led to the far-reaching split between the C.I.O. and the A.F.o.L. In Britain, the issue of industrial *versus* craft Unionism is complicated by the challenge of general Unions, appealing specially to the unskilled and semi-skilled workers in all industries. It will obviously be of the greatest importance to the whole future of Trade Unionism in Germany on what lines its beginning is made. What is the answer?

As an advocate of Industrial Unionism it pleases me to find that of the thirteen Unions in Hamburg, twelve are based on industry. The thirteenth (unlucky number) is a General Workers Union, which, whilst it caters for certain skilled workers, mainly recruits semi-skilled and unskilled labour. At the risk of boring readers who are not interested in Trade Unionism (let them skip this section, if they will), I am going into this matter a little further.

If we in Britain had to start our Trade Union Movement all over again, how should we do it? How should we reorganise our one thousand Trade Unions?* How have our German comrades done it? How have they classified the whole economy so as to get *twelve* industries out of it? Here's the Hamburg solution—I give the membership as well as the "covering" of the Union:

Hamburg Trade Unions and Membership

Transport and Municipal Workers	30,774
Metal Workers	25,209
Employees ("Black-coated")	22,472
Railwaymen	14,357
Factory, Chemicals, Leather and Pottery Workers	10,435
Building Workers	10,000
Food and Drink Workers	6,248
Woodworkers	3,420
Printing and Paper Workers	2,792
Hotel, Restaurant and Café-employees	1,915
Agriculture and Forestry Workers	1,121
Tobacco Workers	975
Clothing and Textile Workers	757
Total (March 31, 1946)	130,475

* This includes many small and insignificant Unions. The Unions affiliated to the British T.U.C. are about one-fourth of this number.

13

All these Unions are co-ordinated in an Administrative Committee for Hamburg—in effect, a Trades Council. It is this Committee which has organised the May Day demonstration for Wednesday and which has invited me to speak. I shall be meeting the Committee this afternoon and can get their side of the story, but this Mil. Gov. report leaves no doubt in my mind as to the genuineness of the rebirth of German Trade Unionism, nor of the value of the contribution which Sherwood is making towards it from his long Trade Union experience. He strikes me as combining solid commonsense with real devotion to the task. I wonder if the Industrial Relations officers in other parts of the British zone are of the same calibre.

POLITICAL ACTIVITY IN GERMANY TO-DAY

Whilst I have been talking with Sherwood, Major Luxton has been fixing appointments for me for to-morrow with Brigadier Armitage, Commander of Hamburg, and Major Hollins, the head of the Food and Agricultural organisation. He has also been doing much besides. I get an impression of the difficulty of holding the balance between the political parties. Karl Meitmann is to broadcast on May Day on behalf of the Trades Council. But, say the Communists, Meitmann is the Social Democratic leader: we demand a speaker also. A deputation from the Communists arrives. Luxton sees them in another room, insisting that Meitmann is speaking as a Trade Unionist and not as a Social Democrat, and that if the Trades Council had chosen a Communist representative he would have spoken. The Communists go away dissatisfied.

Part of the Political Officer's job is to keep a picture in his mind of the political trends in the region. Whilst I am noting particulars of Trade Union development, Luxton receives reports of two of the smaller parties—the Free Democratic Party and the Radical Social Freedom Party. I gather that the Radicalism of the latter may be a camouflage.

Once more I cannot record what Luxton says to me when at last we have an opportunity to talk, but the facts, as supplied by Mil. Gov., show how lively is political activity in the Hamburg region. A record is kept of all public meetings and of Members' meetings with an attendance of over fifty. I note down the return for the previous week (*see next page*).

Why no Communist Members' meetings? Because they meet in "cells" of approximately ten and do not have to report them.

At Karl Meitmann's I have already learned that the strength of the Social Democrats is 24,000 and of the Communists

14

Party.	No. of Public Meetings.	Highest attendance.
Social Democratic Party . .	8	400
Communist Party . . .	5	1,500
Free Democratic Party . .	5	600
Country Party (Lower Saxony) .	4	200
Christian Democratic Party . .	3	500
Republican Party of Germany .	2	100
Radical Social Freedom Party .	1	400
	No. of Members' Meetings.	
Social Democratic Party . .	17	500
Free Democratic Party . .	6	100

14,000. The next largest Parties are the Free Democrats, who can be described as Liberals, with 5,000 and the Christian Democrats (Catholics) with 3,000. I ask about the Country Party. It has only 300 members.

I don't like all this governmental watching of political parties. It's a bit like political espionage, an extended version of our C.I.D. at home, and not the atmosphere for a healthy democracy. But I suppose it is an inevitable function of an Occupying Power, particularly when the growth of Nazism must be guarded against.

The most important impression I get to-day is that the Government is now definitely encouraging the Social Democratic Party. This is a reaction to Russia's support of the Communist Party, and particularly to the dictatorial methods by which it has imposed *Einheit* (fusion) upon the Social Democrats in its zone. I shall collect information about this when I visit Berlin, but the fact of British backing of Democratic Socialism is so important that it should be noted at once. Perhaps it is partly the explanation of the readiness with which I was given permission to speak at the Trade Union demonstration on Wednesday. By the way, I have also been invited to speak at the Social Democrats' May Day demonstration in the afternoon. When I ask whether this is O.K., Mil. Gov. endorsement is given at once and without any restriction on what I shall say.

THE RESORT OF THE OFFICERS

It's time for lunch and I'm invited by a Socialist friend on the economic side of Mil. Gov. to take a meal with him at the

15

Atlantic Hotel. I've already learned the reputation of the Atlantic Hotel. It's the "poshest" place in the city.

We drive back to Alster Lake. As I enter the Atlantic I think I'm in Hollywood. One gets immediately the impression of spacious luxury. The reception counter is thirty feet long; behind it good-looking and efficient German girls will do you any service you want, from finding 'phone numbers to telling you the next plane to Berlin. The lounge is a vast hall, in which uniformed officers, men and women, sit in deep chairs and settees drinking cocktails, which are obediently brought by German waiters. The dining saloons run in a series along the front of the lake, light, airy rooms with well-spaced tables to which guests are conducted by the head-waiter, as though they were the lords of the land. Well, I suppose that is just what we are.*

I have never dined at the Savoy, but I'm sure its famous restaurant could not serve a better meal than we had. I can't help thinking of the people who are walking on the pavement from which we are divided only by a wall. Those people, with one in five starving, whom I watched this morning.

THE PLANS FOR DE-NAZIFICATION

Our subject of conversation is de-Nazification. As soon as he was appointed to Hamburg my friend went to the Socialists and Trade Unionists and asked for a list of all the Nazis holding managerial and administrative posts in the industry for which he was responsible. More important, he asked for a list of people capable of taking over their jobs. Thus when the "de-Nazification" instruction came he was ready.

What were these de-Nazification instructions? I use this lunch-talk to get them clear, deciding to put off until later any investigation as to how far they are working out.

The basis of the plan is a questionnaire which terrifies me as I look at it—twelve pages of questions, divided into nine sections: Personal, Education, Professional or Trade Examinations, Record of Employment and Military Service, Membership of Organisations, Part Time Service with Other Organisations, Writings and Speeches, Income and Assets, Travel or Residence

* Five hundred officers are accommodated at the Atlantic. Later, a visitor told me that he had enquired for the Reading Room. There was none. He enquired for newspapers, British or German. There were none. Finally he was shown the Writing Room, well-furnished with about fifty chairs and writing desks. At no time of the day did he see anyone using this room. He gets the impression that it is entirely a place to "eat, drink and be merry."

Abroad. There are over 400 questions. . . . Phew! I have a feeling that anyone who completed it would have expatiated the worst of offences and qualified for the most exhausting of posts.

Certainly full replies to this questionnaire would enable one to know its subject inside out. Height, weight, colour of hair and eyes, scars, religion, crimes, etc. The names of fifty-seven organisations are given and the examinee is asked to say whether he has belonged to any of them; if so, for how long; and what offices have been held. Space is also left "to specify any other association, society, fraternity, union, syndicate, chamber, institute, group, corporation, club, or other organisation of any kind, whether social, political, professional, educational, cultural, industrial or commercial, with which you have ever been connected or associated even in an honorary capacity". A series of questions ask for income particulars from 1931 to 1945, so that a check can be made on how far the victim of this examination profited from the Nazi régime even if he did not belong to any organisation. There is also a series of questions to enable anti-Nazis to say to what parties or groups they belonged and whether they have taken any part in the underground movement. I can only congratulate the author of this questionnaire on his encyclopædic thoroughness. Surely there has never been anything like it in the world before.*

The answers to these questionnaires, my friend tells me, are examined first by Security Officers, so that dangerous Nazis may be interned; but, after that, I am surprised to hear, they are referred to *German* committees for recommendations as to whether personnel shall be displaced or appointed. The official theory is that all persons shall be removed from public and semi-public office, and from positions of responsibility in important private undertakings, when they have been "more than nominal participants" in the Nazi Party or who are "hostile to Allied purposes". ("What *are* these purposes?" I ask my friend, but he ignores the interruption, except to smile.) They are to be replaced by persons "who, by their political and moral qualities, are deemed capable of assisting in developing genuine democratic institutions in Germany". Except in the

* On my way back in the plane from Hamburg to Croydon I chanced to sit next to an official whose duty it had been to check the accuracy of the replies to this questionnaire. He amazed me by saying that out of 7,000 questionnaires, only 215 had proved false, and these mostly in minor particulars. The task of checking had proved comparatively easy because the Nazi organisations had not destroyed their records, which gave complete case histories of all their members.

cases of arrant Nazis who make themselves objectionable or who wield influence, no one is removed below the foreman grade.

Who are these German authorities who do the sifting? The Hamburg City Council (now a nominated body, but to be elected soon) names the members of a Central De-Nazification panel, which in turn names a series of Functional Panels to cover the major departments of civil administration, the professions, the major groups of industry and commerce. The Council also nominates a Review Board, to whom dismissed persons can appeal. The Panels and Review Board, it is laid down, shall consist of "those sections of the community, such as left-wing parties, Church groups, etc., which have suffered under the Nazis". I'm interested to hear that "Trades Unions and Workers' interests must be predominant". So that the Panels shall have local and personal information, they are assisted in the larger workplaces or in other appropriate groupings by Advisory Committees representative of managements and workers.

On paper this seems to be a very thorough scheme for purging the administration and industry of Nazi officials, but I suspect the snag is in the fact that after the panels have made their recommendations the final decisions rest with the British authorities and that appointments in the Zonal administration cannot be challenged. People in executive posts are always inclined to place a premium on efficiency, and I can imagine them deciding that a Nazi with technical qualifications is preferable every time to a non-Nazi who has to learn his job. This is probably the main difference between the Russian and the British–American approach. Russia says the Nazis must go at any price. The West says we must have efficiency at nearly any price.

The Germans are Mentally Starved

This conversation has been rather hard going. Over coffee we relax and talk of less complicated things. My friend declares that the Germans are just as hungry for mental food as for physical. Their only reading matter are the papers of limited circulation licensed by Mil. Gov., and the information in them is very restricted. They have no modern books of a liberal tendency. The Nazi-minded books of the Hitler period have been destroyed, but they have not so far been replaced by works reflecting the development of democratic thought during the last twelve years. They live in an intellectual vacuum. My friend has personally begun an interesting experiment. He gets the *New Statesman and Nation*, *The Spectator*, *The Tribune*, *Time and Tide*, and the *Listener*, a cross-section of political thought in Britain, binds them together and presents them to a local library. *There is always a queue of Germans waiting for them*, and the librarian states that there is never a moment during the week when they are not being read. This is surely a plan which could be organised on a large scale. I'll have a word with Minister John Hynd about it when I return to London.

It is time for my next appointment. The bill for our two meals is 5*s*. For tip my friend leaves two cigarettes, which the waiter evidently regards as generous. Top black-market prices for cigarettes are 5*s*. each. I haven't eaten my roll, and want to take it to give to the next German I meet. My friend points to a pocket inside my tunic which I have not discovered. I look round to see whether my fellow-diners are looking, and pop the roll in.

A German Woman Pacifist

I drive to the flat of Frau Hoppstock Huth, whom I have known by reputation for twenty years as a pacifist and humanist, one of the outstanding women of the old Germany. She was the Secretary of the Women's International League and active in many good causes. I wonder how she had fared as a Pacifist under the Nazi régime and during the war.

She lives in a middle-class district, occupying a flat on the second floor of a large house. She is a tall, slim, middle-aged woman, intellectual and giving an impression of a calm, strong character; but she is human and friendly. Her small sitting-room is crowded, with unusual "arty" pictures and photo-gravures standing on her document-covered desk and her full bookshelves, and with a bowl of lilac on the table. She is excited to see me, and asks eagerly after mutual friends in England and America. I take the roll of bread from my pocket and place it on the table. She protests, but she leaves it there.

Frau Huth is a member of the Hamburg City Council. There are eighty-two members, fifty-nine of them appointed to represent the various parties—Social Democrats, Communists, Free Democrats, Christian Democrats—and the Trades Unions. There is a "Party-less" group of twenty-three, mostly industrial and financial figures, anti-socialist in attitude. Seven of the Council are women.

Her main activity apparently is associated with the Ex-Political Prisoners' Group. She herself was in prison and concentration camps from May, 1944, to April, 1945. She remarks that she is fortunate to be alive: the woman in the flat above her was executed by the Nazis a month before the German capitulation. I get a picture of how the Gestapo worked. Suspecting the woman above, they put a spy into her flat ostensibly as a comrade. Frau Huth is bitter because the spy (after a few months in prison) is now at liberty and boasting of her freedom.

She makes light of her past sufferings, however, and of her present deprivations. As an anti-Nazi prisoner she has an extra ration—1300 calories a day instead of the 1048 minimum. But, whilst she brushes aside her own difficulties, she speaks movingly of the struggle which others have. She tells of a woman whom she had met that morning who was trying to exchange a cupful of milk for bread because her children were crying for food. She tells of a veteran of the woman suffrage movement who is deteriorating physically before her eyes, thinner and more haggard each day.

The people get no potatoes, and only a fragment of meat each week. What do they eat? I ask. Mostly turnips, but there is no fat to cook them in and the turnips are so tough that it is impossible to grate them. Then how are they eaten? As soup, but there is no barley to add to them. The soup is horrible; but still it is something to eat.

A Teacher and Her Pupils

At this point there is a knock at the door and another woman enters. She is small and pinched, a school teacher. She exclaims when she sees the roll of bread, and Frau Huth immediately insists that she takes it. "You know I have extra rations," she persuades. The school teacher has a class in a secondary school, forty girls between twelve and fourteen years of age. Of the forty, six or seven are absent each week through hunger-weakness. The previous week four children had not come. She went to their home to enquire, and found the children in bed, too weak to walk. There was no bread, meat, porridge in the house—not even a turnip.

Frau Huth says that the overcrowding which has followed the bomb-destruction makes the strain of the hunger worse. People's nerves are all in tangles, first because their stomachs are empty, second because they are all on top of each other. She instances two families of eleven persons who are living in three small rooms, and a mother and eleven children who occupy two rooms, with the father expected back daily from a

Prisoner of War camp. (As I listen I say to myself that we could parallel this in Britain; but we haven't the hunger to make it worse.) Frau Huth describes a home which she visited the day before. A family of six—parents and four children—occupying one room. Between them they had eight slices of bread a day. A little girl of five was eating dry bread. A neighbour bustled in with a great prize—some rancid fat. A little was spread on the child's bread. "I like it," she exclaimed delightedly.

The teacher begins to talk of her school again. The only books are primers for children between six and seven. There are no exercise books : children bring the edge of newspapers to write on. No history lessons are allowed at present, but she speaks enthusiastically of a new history book which is being prepared. Then she makes an extraordinary statement. She remembers what teaching was like when the Social Democrats were in charge of Hamburg before Hitler : the curriculum was the most advanced in Germany. She had hoped that under British supervision education would go back to that; but no. Education is being introduced on the old English Public School lines—"like your Etons and Harrows" : dead languages rather than modern science. She instanced a class of girls of sixteen. They have, she said, six lessons weekly in Latin, four lessons in Greek, and only two in natural sciences. There are two lessons weekly in religion, from which parents can "contract out" their children. This sounds to me extraordinary, and I make a note to enquire about it.

Before I go we talk of longer prospects. I am surprised to hear these women speaking of the German people in much the way Lord Vansittart shocked us by doing. They are pessimistic about them, would be glad to live in another country. I think again—and am not so surprised. I have heard British pacifists speak of the British people in much the same strain—they are "more concerned about football than starvation in Europe". I can't think of either the German people or the British people in this way. My experience is that the average man or woman in all countries is fundamentally decent, wanting nothing more than to live in peace and security, wanting that for themselves and others.

A Talk With Hamburg Trades Council

Karl Meitmann arrives to take me to meet the Hamburg Trades Council. It occupies the old building of the Nazi Labour Front—the free Trade Unionists took possession on the day the German armies withdrew.* As I sit down at a large board-room table I try to imagine the scene a year ago, with the Nazi Labour Front Fuehrers occupying the seats which these typical Trade Unionists now fill. They *are* typical Trade Unionists, just the same type who run our Trades Councils in Britain—a transport worker, an engineer, a docker, a tobacco worker, a compositor, an agricultural labourer, a building worker. I feel at home.

The oldest member and chairman is a tall lean man with a pointed beard. I half remember him, and then he holds out his hand and says, "We met in Berlin in the thirties". He is Franz Spliedt, one of the old school of pre-Hitler Trade Unionists. The youngest member is dark, keen-featured, direct and clear in speech, reminding me of Emmanuel Shinwell thirty years ago. He is one of the two secretaries of the Council —Wil Peterson and Ernst Rathlow—to tell you the truth, I am not sure which. At the head of the table is Kummernuss, the transport workers' leader, a tall, heavily-built man. We settle down for a talk.

I ask what are the most urgent issues in their minds. At once and all round the table they say: *Give the Trades Unions and the Workers' Councils some real power.* At present they have only advisory functions; they cannot negotiate about wages, except within very small limits; they have no control of conditions in the workplaces. Whilst this limitation persists they can hardly be called Trades Unions.

Their second answer moves me. It is a plea rather than a demand—an appeal for international association with their fellow Trade Unionists in other lands. These men feel their isolation, their boycott, very keenly. They are ashamed of Germany's record, but they themselves (or most of them) have no need for shame. They have put up a fight against Nazism in concentration camps, prisons, torture chambers, which few Trades Unionists of other countries can equal in courage.

Their next request is linked with this: that I shall tell British Trade Unionists on my return how Free Trade Unionism has been reborn and grown strong in Germany. They want this to be known because they believe that a powerful Trade Union Movement in Germany is the surest guarantee of enduring democracy and peace.

Only after these pleas for status and recognition do I hear a

* Later I am told that when the Trade Unionists first took over the building they were turned out by the military. This was before the Unions were made legal.

22

reference to material demands. The first is food. The second is work. Unless more food comes, they say, Germany will go back to reaction, democracy will be defeated. They are very moderate in their demands; they recognise the world food shortage, but ask that the German people shall be given enough food to live without physical deterioration so that they can make their contribution to recovery. The question of work is related to the extent to which Germany is to be allowed to retain her industries. They do not ask that war industries shall remain, but they plead that industries which may be useful for peace shall continue. They do not mention Hamburg ship-building, but I have no doubt it is in their minds.

Our talk becomes more general. I hear two startling statements. One of the things which has impressed me about Hamburg is its trees: they line the streets and fill the parks and gardens. But one of these men says that Hamburg and its neighbouring forests will be denuded next winter if some fuel is not available.* The second assertion which startles me is the allegation that 1,200 tons of tea are lying unused in Hamburg warehouses. Yet the people of the city, allowed only a trifling ration of ersatz coffee, are thirsting for tea.

Before I go I make one request: may I have a copy of the poster of the coming May Day demonstration as a souvenir? They immediately get the artists' original design—green and red on a white background—and all of them sign it. These are its slogans: *"For Peace and Freedom—For Laws to Protect the Workers—For Planned Reconstruction of the Economic Life—For Equality of the Workers in the Economic System—For a New United Germany as a Member of a Big Family of Nations."*†

A Talk with Socialist Doctors

I am tired at the end of this interview. Since first thing in the morning my mind has been an unrelaxed recording instrument, and the emotion of being in the midst of physical hunger has made me overwrought. I am now to visit the home of a socialist medical man, Dr. Hecht, who had been a member of the German I.L.P., the Socialist Workers' Party (S.A.P.), and who now belongs, with his former comrades, to the Left Group in the Social Democratic Party. My soldier friend is waiting for me outside the Trade Union headquarters, and Karl Meitmann

* The wooden slats on public seats in recreation grounds have all gone. It is strange to see people sitting only on the iron supports at each end.

† Both the Trades Council and the Tobacco Workers' Union afterwards gave me pipes as souvenirs.

drives me to the distant suburb in which the doctor lives. I look forward to a cosy, domestic hour where I can "let up" a bit.

The door of a neat little house is opened by a charming young woman, the doctor's wife, and the doctor himself bursts into a hall, overflowing with comradeship.* This is encouraging. Then he shepherds me and my soldier friend into his surgery (Meitmann has had to go back)—and my anticipations of a light, domestic hour fade. There are three men awaiting me looking formidably like a deputation. I adjust myself, but I'm afraid I don't succeed in hiding my irritation. I really am too tired to listen.

The two elder men are doctors. The young man has come to see me urgently about his brother who is interned. He is of a type with which I am familiar in Britain—face glowing with earnestness and fraternity: I bet he's a rebel against the conventions, content with little for to-day and never planning for to-morrow. His name proves to be Theodor Bergman; before Hitler he had belonged to the Communist Opposition in Berlin. He went in 1939 to Sweden, where he was recognised as a political refugee. On April 1 of this year he returned to Germany voluntarily with his brother, Josef. He was allowed by the British to enter, but Josef has been detained and is still in an internment camp. Theodor suspects the British think he is an agent of the Communist International, though, in fact, he has never been a member of the Communist Party or of any Communist-controlled organisation. I promise to raise the matter with the British. I ask for the names of people who can vouch for his brother, and get a list which should certainly do the trick.†

* Later I learn the interesting story of Mrs. Hecht. During the war Dr. Hecht was discharged from the army by the Nazis as "politically unreliable". He was compelled to do forced labour in Brussels, fell in love with one of two Belgian sisters, and married her at the end of the war. The Belgian military police then came to Hamburg and arrested her for "collaborating with the Germans" because of her association with Dr. Hecht. She was in prison for some months before being acquitted. Her sister was not so fortunate. She has been sentenced to three years' imprisonment, because of her German fiancé. I have written to my old friend, Minister Spaak, about her case.

† At my request, John Hynd has initiated enquiries about this case. At the time of writing Josef is interned in a camp for Nazi suspects. The father of Theodor and Josef was Rabbi of the largest synagogue of Berlin—its Jewish "cathedral". He had six sons. They all became Socialists or Communist "Oppositionists". One of the sons died in a concentration camp during the war. (*Later:* Bergman has been released.)

The doctor who speaks first is middle-aged, with the lined face of a man who has faced extreme adversity. He wants to enlist my help in getting the British authorities to import soya beans. Now, soya beans happen to be a complex with me, because of an incident in the life of one of my children. When she was an infant we could not find a food which she could digest: she was fretful night and day. Then someone suggested soya milk, and lo and behold, it worked a miracle: the child became a model for sleep and quietness. I became a soya enthusiast—until the child became too quiet. We called in a doctor, and he told us that she was starved.

I am rude enough to tell this story now. The doctor shakes his head and is sure that something is wrong with my account. My host interrupts to say that the speaker is one of Germany's first dietitians. I regret my rudeness and listen carefully. Soya beans, the doctor tells me, possess from 36 to 40 per cent of a protein which, although of vegetable origin, contains equally with meat, eggs and the casein of milk all the amino acids which the human body requires to build up its own protein. He compares the nutritive value of wheat and soya beans. One thousand tons of wheat contain 3,000 millions of calories. One thousand tons of soya beans contain 3,700. The protein content of 1,000 tons of wheat is 120,000 kilos; of 1,000 tons of soya beans, 360,000 kilos. Moreover, the wheat protein is of inferior quality, whilst the soya protein is "complete" in the biological sense of the word. It also has the advantage that it can be offered for consumption in popular forms, such as milk and sausages.

I ask whether the collection and transport of soya beans would be as easy as of wheat. The cost of supplies to fill an equal cargo space, the doctor says, would be 14 per cent higher for soya beans, but the caloric value would be 23·3 per cent higher and the protein content 200 per cent higher. As for available supplies, he admits that the damage done by the war in the Far East is a severe handicap, but new soya-bean acreages have been developed in other parts of the world. The United States, for example, are reported to dispose of annual crops of about 5,000,000 tons. In Germany, unfortunately, the stores of seeds were destroyed in 1944.

What would 1,000 tons of soya beans mean in concrete terms for Germany? I ask. They would enable 165,000 children to have half a litre of extra milk per day—and the protein content would be 5·6 per cent, as against 3·5 per cent in cow's milk. *In addition*, 140,000 patients in German hospitals, which at present have no effective means to cure malnutrition cases, could have 50 grams of high-value protein extra per day.

An idea occurs to me. Can I visit a hospital and *see* the malnutrition cases? The faces around me light with gratitude and hope. Certainly. We fix it for Wednesday afternoon.

The doctor feels that my scepticism has gone. He speaks with even greater earnestness. "There is no other raw material in the world," he says, "from which such high results can be obtained at such low expenditure of cargo space, money and manufacturing cost. I do not believe that the hunger problem of Germany can be solved by any means except by international action to produce and distribute soya beans." He stops, and then adds a striking phrase. "It is beyond doubt," he declares, "that the soya bean will revolutionise modern diet in the same way that the introduction of potatoes in the eighteenth century and of margarine in the nineteenth enlarged and cheapened the basis of nutrition to the benefit of the masses." I am impressed and promise that when I get back to London I will put the case to John Hynd.*

Nazis Still Run the Medical Service

The third spokesman is also a doctor, the oldest of the three, impressive. I look interested as I hear his subject—the de-Nazification of the medical service. Already I'm to have the opportunity to put to the test the paper-scheme explained to me at lunch. He tells me that a Commission had been set up to de-Nazify doctors and surgeons, but according to him it is a farce. He alleges that the President of the Hamburg Board of Health was a member of the Nazi Party from 1922 to 1931. He then quarrelled with the Party, but wanted to rejoin in 1937. The Nazis wouldn't have him back, but his enthusiasm for the Party was so great, I am assured, that he compelled all the members of his staff to join it on pain of dismissal. "I can produce three witnesses who were so forced to join the Party," says this doctor.

I find it difficult to understand how Mil. Gov. should appoint such a man head of the health service in Hamburg. The doctor explains. In 1943 this man was imprisoned for writing a letter to his son saying that the war would be lost by Germany. It was this imprisonment which won him the confidence of the British authorities.

I ask them why they have not raised the matter with Mil.

* Mr. John Hynd and Mr. John Strachey are both considering whether means can be found to transport soya beans to Germany.

Gov. "We cannot speak to the British Medical authorities except through the President of the Hamburg Board of Health," says the first. "From the President downwards there is a prejudice against members of the Social Democratic Party," says the second. The third says: "No Socialist comes to any position in the medical service. Only Nazis."

Is this the same in other services and in industry? I enquire. In some, not in others. They mention petrol and electricity as two industries in which de-Nazification has been carried out thoroughly, but say that in many other trades the Nazi "big bugs" remain even when the small ones have been weeded out. They cite an important undertaking as an example, asserting that the Nazis have been left in control. Only one technician has been dismissed—and he is an anti-Nazi!

The conversation broadens out. They are angry about housing, alleging that Mil. Gov. turned people out of their homes with unnecessary ruthlessness when it required premises for housing troops and staff or for offices. There was a restriction upon the removal of furniture, yet it had afterwards been thrown into back yards and allowed to rot. They say that the people are losing their faith in Mil. Gov. because of dishonesties they are finding in propaganda. I ask for an example, and they tell me of an official campaign to mobilise bicycles. In Hamburg the people were told that bicycles were needed to enable miners to reach the pits to get coal: in the Ruhr the people were told that they were needed to enable dockers to reach the ships to unload food. When I express incredulity, they assure me that these statements were broadcast over the radio and in the press.

Two unrelated points come out in this conversation:

1. *There has been a 30 per cent increase in open T.B. cases: that is, cases who cough bacillus. (T.B., these doctors take for granted, is primarily caused by hunger and bad housing.) And there is no pure paraffin available in Germany to enable the operation of collapsing lungs to be carried out.**

2. *The war has wiped out the greater part of the masculine youth of Germany. For example, in Lichtenrade, a suburb of Berlin, where a sample test was taken, in a population of 15,000 there were only eighty-one male youths between sixteen and twenty-one years of age.*

I rise to go. The oldest doctor puts his hand on my sleeve to detain me. "One word more," he says. "The root trouble with the Military Government is that it has no plan, no positive policy. The German people know that food, housing, fuel

* I took this up with Mr. Hynd. In August he assured me that paraffin was available for all hospitals.

cannot be solved in a day. They know that de-Nazification is complicated by the need to retain and train technicians. They wouldn't complain—if they saw a thought-out plan in what the Military Government is doing. They would follow a plan. But this 'muddling through', these hand-to-mouth devices, this compromising and chaos are destroying our faith and hope. I beg of you to tell your people in London that."

It is getting on for eight when I leave with my soldier friend, and for once we have no car. As we walk to the electric line station, we pass a large block of modern flats. It has been taken over completely for troops. "Where are the displaced families living?" I ask. "We'll show you some of Hamburg's homeless to-night," he replies. In the train we discuss how we shall get a meal: it is too late for food at our mess and there are no public restaurants. My friend will get what he can at a NAAFI. I will try Streit's and if necessary the Atlantic Hotel, though I hate its luxurious atmosphere. We arrange that he shall look me up at both before we start on our night's adventure.

A Major Surprises Me

The last meal has been served at Streit's, and at first it looks as though I am too late at the Atlantic. When I go to some high official, however, I am ushered into the restaurant despite the notice "CLOSED" on the door. I have a meal such as I have not tasted since before the war. Opposite me, at a table for two, is a major. I am a little hesitant in opening the conversation, until he says suddenly: "I don't know how we swallow this food when God knows whether there'll be any bread for these German people in ten days' time." He tells me an extraordinary experience. He has been on leave in Denmark and Sweden. In Denmark there is a glut of meat. Farmers have been told not to slaughter cattle, and the merchants have stocks of meat and bacon which they cannot sell. It is the same with fish. In both Denmark and Sweden they have so much that they don't know what to do with it. The Swedish fish merchants offered to sell their surplus to the hungry countries in Europe at half the market price, but the offer was declined, so they have thrown two-thirds of their catch back into the sea.* The major on the opposite side of the table is more explosive about this than I could possibly be.

* I made enquiries about these assertions later and was informed that the food offered consisted of "left-overs", and that even so the fish could not be used because there were no arrangements for refrigeration or for transporting it. I was not entirely satisfied with this explanation.

Our conversation is interrupted by laughter from neighbouring tables. It is spreading through the restaurant. I look up. Germans have a better method than ours of "pageing" in hotels and clubs. They don't send a small boy through the rooms shouting a name in a shrill voice. They send him round silently carrying a blackboard bearing the name of the person required. Such a board is now being carried between our tables. I read the name—"Mr. Buggery"—and join in the laughter. Then an awful thought occurs to me. Is "Mr. Buggery" intended to be me? I pay my bill, leave two cigarettes as tip, and go out to the reception office to enquire. "Brockway?" says the German clerk. "Perhaps that's it—your driver is here, sir."

My "driver" is my soldier friend. The only "other ranks" who can get into this exclusive hotel are drivers awaiting their officer passengers, and they have to wait in a lobby. I cause comment by taking my "driver's" arm and swinging through the doors with him in uproarious laughter as I tell him the story of "Mr. Buggery". Probably I am excused as drunk.

Visit to the Black Market District

We walk through the dark streets to the station. Men slink up to us and whisper. They remind me of the pimps in Paris who seek for customers for brothels. But these are cigarette pimps. "Five marks for a cigarette," they insinuate. They are working for a 100 per cent profit; the black market price is ten marks. We travel by electric to St. Pauli, which my friend tells me is the criminal and black market area of Hamburg. We are to go to the police station, where my doctor host of this evening is the Divisional Surgeon: we ought to learn something. When we emerge from the station I see heavy bomb damage for the first time, but it is dark and the destruction does not appear to be more than I've seen in England. "You wait," says my soldier friend again.

At the police station we talk to an official whilst waiting for the doctor. I ask about the black market and hear something which surprises me. The greatest source of supply, I am told, is UNRRA, which has the responsibility of feeding the non-Germans. The population in the UNRRA camps is a mixed lot, this police official says, with a high proportion of adventurers and people who have been demoralised by their experience over the last six years. Their ration is higher than outside, and when big money can be made by the sale of food it is inevitable that there should be trafficking in it. The official hints that the UNRRA staff is not free from guilty individuals. Another considerable source of supply of goods is the army, though not so large as might be expected. Then there is illicit trade with the country districts and across the frontiers from Denmark and Holland. Sometimes large supplies of imports get lost—to turn up later in the black market. Besides all this, there is a lot of casual and amateur black marketing—individuals trading personal valuables with food distributors. Cigarettes have become a medium of exchange in this trade almost as extensive as money.

THE SHELTERS GERMANS STILL LIVE IN

The doctor comes out of his office, with a young German who is introduced to me as a comrade. The doctor tells me we are too late to see anything except the shelter accommodation, and I begin to think the journey has been a waste of time. Nevertheless, I want to see how the homeless, the bombed out and the dispossessed are existing.

We descend a decline from the street, much like the entrance to underground shelters at home. We don't get far when a wave of foul air hits us. I've never believed that air could hit, but this is like a wall, which stops me going on. It gets into my lungs, and I cough and cough and fear I am going to be sick. Then I suppose I become accustomed to it, and go on, breathing thickly but not noticing the foulness so much. We come to a passage with doors on either side. The doctor opens one, and we are in a concrete tomb, about fifteen feet by twelve. On one side are berths like those which were in the London tubes during the war, four sets with three berths above each other. On the other side is a long table, used for eating. Eleven men are sleeping in the berths: one man is reading a newspaper at the table. We do not go into a women's tomb. The doctor tells me that four women share a "room" six feet by six.

He asks whether we would like to go to the lower floors. Lower floors? Yes, there are two more. I want to get out of this stinking place as soon as possible and, when the doctor says the rooms are similar to the one we've entered, I'm prepared to leave it at that. I notice a men's lavatory. I swing the door open, expecting to be revolted, but the lavatory is clean with water-flushing. I climb as rapidly to the surface as I can, and when I get into the fresh air breathe deeply again and again and again. I feel I will never get the foul air out of my system, that my breath will smell for a month. I do not wonder that tuberculosis is mounting in Hamburg.

We catch the last train back, and I have to walk two miles to the Warcormess. The young German Socialist whom I met at the police station shows me the way. The streets are empty, because it is past curfew hour. My young friend is committing an offence, but he says he would risk much more than this to have a talk with me. He opens his heart. He is starved, not so much physically as mentally and spiritually. He has hardly read a socialist book—just a few Marxist classics of the pre-Hitler period, which older comrades had buried in the ground. He hasn't been able to read, because no modern books are available. His longing to learn is pathetic: he asks me a hundred questions, about new ideas, about the movement in Britain and in other countries. He wants intensely to fit himself for the socialist task in Germany, and he feels inadequate. I would have liked to walk the night through with this lad, but both of us have to be up early in the morning. As we say good-bye, I realise how urgent is this need for intellectual food in Germany.

THE THIRD DAY

April 30th, 1946.

A cup of tea is brought to my bed at six-thirty by the smiling German maid and she tells me an early breakfast will be served for me specially in the "summer-room" at seven. The summer-room is a conservatory filled with the morning sun. Two eggs are on my plate. I put one in my pocket for Grete. In addition, there are fruit, toast, fresh butter and marmalade.*

Before eight the car is speeding me round the lake-side to the home of Karl Meitmann. The broad stretch of water, the trees, the gardens and large houses drug one to the feeling that all is well with the world . . . until one sees a woman passing from dustbin to dustbin in search of food.

I have brought my civvies with me, and change into them when I get to Karl's. So far I've only been hearing about the German people. Now I'm going to hear what they say themselves. I am going into their homes to see their conditions. I am going to talk to them on their jobs. My uniform must be discarded if I am to break down the barrier between conquerors and conquered. Karl's son, Jack, has organised the programme. He and Heinz Heydorn, Hamburg's Socialist Youth leader, come with me.

VISIT TO WORKING-CLASS HOMES

We walk a few streets and push open the door of a large house which has gone shabby. We knock at a door on the ground floor, and a woman, drab and tired, invites us in. It's a large room, carpetless, with wall-paper falling down, dark because the bombed-out windows are boarded. There is a large cracked wardrobe and two iron bedsteads, not yet tidied up. Against a wall I am surprised to see a pile of blocks of wood. The woman explains that she is given 100 lbs. a month because her husband died in Dachau concentration camp. She has three children. One is clinging to her skirts, a fair little girl with a head of untidy curls. The Social Welfare Committee

---

* I made a practice of secreting food at every meal. Once I forgot that an egg was in a hip pocket, with disastrous results to my clothing!

has sent the two others to the country because they were ill with under-nourishment.

She cannot work because of a weak heart. I ask her how she lives. The Welfare Committee allows her 100 marks a month— 12s. 6d. a week. She adds a few shillings by letting a small room to an Italian woman and her child. She is on the 1048 calorie ration and both her child and herself are often hungry, though the child gets some food from the Swedish Red Cross. We look in the second room; it is not much more than a cupboard and again the window is boarded in. The Italian woman and her child are still asleep. The two women share a kitchen.

The woman has spoken quietly, accepting her lot as fate. Suddenly she speaks with venom and her eyes blaze. "The Nazi swine who denounced my man to the Gestapo," she exclaims, "the man who sent him to Dachau, sent him to his death—he is now an official of the Welfare Service, which doles out charity to me." I am startled. I will enquire about this.*

It's a long time since I have seen such a wretched home as the second we visit; indeed, I have only seen anything worse in Bombay. We go down into the basement of another house. I can't see my way, but a woman opens the door of what looks like an underground cellar and a dim light breaks through. There had been a window, but it is entirely blocked up with bricks. The woman is weary-faced, but she and everything about her is clean and she is self-reliant and courageous. Her man was killed in action, her five children are all away, she has another coming. The furniture on a stone floor consists of a bed, a cot, a small table, and a wood-burning stove. The stove is of a type supplied by the City Council—it stands on four narrow legs like a table, an iron box in which the wood is burned, with a hole in the cover for kettle or saucepan. She recites the items of her miserable 1048 calorie ration and says she has now become accustomed to constant hunger. She can hardly remember when she last had a hot meal. She is worried because she can't get brushes to keep her room clean.

She is still more worried because she has notice to quit. There are two unused rooms and they are wanted for a family with children. I go into these "rooms". They are dungeons, with no ventilation, not even boarded-in windows, so dark that we have to light a match to see. I think of the lovely house where I had breakfast in the summer-room this morning. One cannot believe in sunshine and flowers here. I feel it would be a crime for children to be housed here—and then I remember the foul .

* I have not yet had the information.

shelter I visited last night. I wonder whether any children were there.

A Middle-Class Home

Our next visit is to a middle-class home. The man and his wife, middle-aged, are Social Democrats and give us a friendly welcome. He had been for two and a half years in Oldenburg and Teufelsmoor concentration camps and tells me that the present ration is almost identical with what he received there. His clothes hang baggily and he tells me he has lost 80 lbs. in weight in a year. He shows me photographs of himself and his wife a year ago. It is almost impossible to believe that they are the same people. He gives me statistics I have not heard before. In 1939, 35 per cent of the people of Hamburg were above standard weight and 25 per cent below. Now between 70 and 75 per cent are below. Weights have dropped steeply since 1942, but never so steeply as now. He is a craftsman-painter, but finds that he is too feeble to carry on for more than six hours a day. He used to do eight and nine hours easily. The woman tells me that if she does housework for a few hours a black veil seems to come before her eyes and she has to hold on to something to prevent herself falling.

Their small flat is crowded with furniture and the woman apologises for the confusion. The man is bitter because, on twenty-four hours' notice, they were turned out of their former home to accommodate British troops. Most of those turned out were allowed only to take bed, bedding and what they could carry. He and his wife were allowed to remove their furniture because he had been in a concentration camp.

Talk With Demolition Workers

We go out into the streets. I see men working on a demolition job and approach one of them. Four others gather round. They tell me that they get extra rations for hard work. This is what the extra amounts to :—

First and third weeks: 3⅛ oz. meat, 12½ oz. bread.
Second and fourth weeks: 4¹¹⁄₁₆ oz. meat, 3⅜ oz. bread, 7¹³⁄₁₆ oz. oatmeal.

They say that with this addition to the 1048 calories daily they still periodically become faint when at work. How often depends on one's constitution, but sooner or later they all experience it. Few of them can work four hours without becoming dizzy. They do a forty-eight-hour working week—the

34

heaviest work is only forty hours—and are paid 91 pfennigs (11*d.*) an hour. Do they belong to their Trade Union? No, not yet.

They are under the impression that the food situation in Hamburg is the worst in Germany. They can do without fat and vegetables, but potatoes and bread are "the substance of life". In the Russian zone, they say, people get potatoes and bread, and because of this there is a tendency among the workers to move over to the Communist Party. I question them all about this, and they agree.

Jack Meitmann says we must get on. We jump on a crowded tramcar—the trams always seem crowded to the very footboards—and go into the centre of the city. Heinz asks me whether I would like to see the black market at work. We enter a side street: men are standing about, singly and in groups. That appears to be all. Then one notices two men standing close to each other, conversing. Something passes between them—a box of cigarettes, a watch, a brooch. Paper money passes in return. They separate, and one walks sharply away. That is all.

A Displaced Persons' Camp

We are to pick up a car at the City Council chambers. I'm introduced there to Senator Nevermann, a young Socialist administrator, giving the impression of ability. I'm not sure what "Senator" signifies.* Another Socialist, Elsner by name, once a member of the Socialist Workers' Party, accompanies us in the car.

They tell me we are bound for a Displaced Persons' camp. I am not eager to go—not because it will not be interesting to see, but because I can't investigate everything in Germany in fourteen days and I had not included displaced persons in my agenda. Certainly the visit proves interesting. The camp is on a large open space on the outskirts of Hamburg—I am told it was the scene of May Day demonstrations in the pre-Hitler days. It is a desolate place now, rows of Nissen Huts without any relief of trees or gardens. The people here are Germans who have come from the Russian zone and want to return. The camp can accommodate 5,000: there are 2,700 in residence. They are supposed to stay only forty-eight hours, but in fact they have been here for two weeks. It is rumoured that the frontier of the Russian zone is closed.

The midday meal is being distributed, and the inmates are

* I am told that a Senator is equivalent to a Minister. The City Council has the status of a State Parliament. At present its members are nominated.

lined up with bowls outside the kitchen. The meal consists of soup. They insist that I taste; it's satisfying, but I cannot say it's tasty. The ingredients are white cabbage, soya bean, and a little meat. I look in at one of the men's huts. There are thirty-two men, lying on rugs or ground-sheets on straw. The men complain that there isn't enough straw. I speak to the Commander of the camp about this. He tells me that he had tried to put in beds, but Mil. Gov. seized them. He had then bought extra supplies of straw from an island in the Baltic. That had been seized by Mil. Gov., too. I look in at a women's hut. The women are also thirty-two to a hut, but have wooden bunks, one above another.

One corner of the camp is given over to another kind of "displaced person"—the wives of Nazis who have been interned by Mil. Gov. One of them accosts me, a self-confident, hard-voiced woman. Her husband had been on the Embassy staff at Buenos Aires since 1922, but she assures me that for him it was only a civil service job. He wasn't a politician. "The small men from Buenos Aires are held," she complains, "whilst the big men are released." I promise to make enquiries.* We rejoin our car.

Whole Working-Class Area Destroyed

Several times I have remarked that bomb damage in Hamburg did not appear to be worse than in many English cities. The retort has always been: Wait and see. Now I do see. We drive to what was the largest working-class area in the town—and find it entirely gone. For literally miles there is hardly a house standing and those which stand are not more than skeletons. Yet I am wrong. This waste used to be the scene of a socialist housing scheme, second in reputation in the twenties only to the Marx, Engels and Reumann Hofs of Vienna. And here, in the midst of all the gaping walls and rubble, stands a beautiful modern school, entirely undamaged. As I look, astonished, the children begin to come out. They clamber over heaps of stones and bricks, their satchels fastened firmly on their backs, making their way to the homes which are still to be found in the cellars underneath all this destruction. I think that picture of the school and the children in this wilderness of devastation will always remain with me.

We walk in the shadow of these high walls which once were the frontage of dwellings five storeys high. They stand, but everything else above ground has gone. Below ground level,

* I am still awaiting replies.

36

every twenty yards or so, rooms have somehow remained intact. There are clean curtains and flowers in the windows—how unconquerable is the human spirit in home-making! We descend steps and knock at a door by chance. Two boys are at home: mother has not come back from shopping; their father?—he is missing on the Russian front. These boys are proud of their home—they and their mother have made it what it is, and they show us the three rooms willingly—whitewashed walls, flowers on the table, a radio playing music, everything spotlessly clean, an impression of light and colour which moves me to wonder.

We return to the car and drive on amidst the ruins. I am silent as I am told of the 46,000 who were killed in three days. Before this I had seen only the wealthier and middle-class districts of Hamburg, the former almost untouched, the latter no worse than London. But nothing in Britain approaches this destruction of the working-class areas of Hamburg—the areas near the factories and docks. Sixty-four per cent of the total *accommodation* of Hamburg was destroyed.

Journalists Say There is No Hunger

I return to Warcormess for lunch. My German friend, Wolf, representing *Forward*, has arrived. Over our meal one of the journalists at the table asks me how I have spent the morning. I tell him. "And what is your conclusion?" he asks. "That unless more food is made available," I reply, "there is no hope of building democracy here." Another journalist breaks in. "Well," he says, "I hear a lot about hunger in Germany, but I've been here three weeks and I've not found a hungry German yet." "Thank you, sir, thank you for saying that," exclaims the officer who presides. "I've been waiting a long time to hear someone say that."

There are two officers and five journalists at the table besides Wolf and me. Except for one officer, all assert that there is no hunger in Germany. I've had a high view of my profession until now. Generally speaking, I have found journalists objective enquirers for facts. But this shocks me. This meal which we have just finished is more than a whole day's ration for nine million Germans in the British zone. And whilst eating it these newspaper men, colleagues of mine, say that they have been unable to find a hungry German.

The Agricultural Chief

At an American aerodrome I once saw two notices over doorways: "Gentlemen—Whites" and "Men—Coloured". This

37

afternoon, in the lavatory at the suite of offices of the Food and Agricultural Department, I find these notices: "Officers", "Other Ranks" and "German Staff". This deserves to live as a classic in class and race snobbery!

I am up against yesterday morning's problem again. To-day I am meeting Major Hollins, head of the Food and Agricultural Department, and then Brigadier Armitage, the Commander of Hamburg and head of the whole administration—and I am not allowed to quote them. Well, for the time being I must content myself with giving my personal impressions.

There is no doubt about the ability of Major Hollins. He would lick to a frazzle any Cabinet Minister at Question Time in the Commons—and without the help of the civil service. He is approaching middle-age, strong-featured, courteous, but always the official. I have the impression that he places technical efficiency first and would be impatient with political obstacles.

An Impression of the Commander

Brigadier Armitage is a very different type—sixtiesh, I should guess, beaming with friendliness, the kind of military man who devotes himself to good works and religious organisations when he retires. We sit and talk for an hour and a half, and, whilst I find that he reflects orthodox views, there is no doubting his sincere desire to do the right thing. When I raise questions on special subjects outside his knowledge, he immediately makes enquiries over the 'phone from the heads of the departments and is as interested in the answers as I am. Sometimes he sends for the responsible officers. He tells me of a scheme for "re-education" through religious clubs, and when I am a little sceptical he brings in a trusted assistant whose duty it is to learn what the German people are thinking. This officer has no doubt about the clubs and stays on to report on other matters. I am a little surprised by what he says—it does not bear out what I have been hearing, but it reassures the Commander. We spend quite a time discussing education in the schools and again the General calls in the head of this department and I get a lot of information. Then I bid farewell to the General. I have respect for his character, even though I differ from his views.

There is Little Unemployment

In the passage outside I meet Sherwood, and he tells me that Mr. Bennett, the head of the Man Power section, would like to see me. I like Bennett: he is a human being before he is an official. In answer to questions he gives me a memo. which provides information which I've been seeking. Part of it is related to the bomb damage I've seen this morning. I find that 47 per cent of the buildings in Hamburg were completely destroyed and 27 per cent partly destroyed. No fewer than 95,000 dwellings were in need of repair; of these, 24,008 have been put right. The number of bombed out people who are living in hutted camps is 3,531; the number who are living in shelter bunks is 2,918.

The other subject about which I have wanted information is unemployment. The figures surprise me. The percentage is only 4·4, and of the 22,000 unemployed only 2,876 are fit for normal employment. Of the 19,786 unemployed men, only 211 are fit for normal work. Despite the idle shipbuilding yards and factories held up for coal, the repairing of Hamburg's war damage, plus other work and services, is providing jobs for practically the whole population.

Before leaving Mil. Gov. headquarters I look in at Major Luxton's office and meet there a well-known Social Democrat from the Russian sector of Berlin. He astonishes me by requesting that his identity shall not be disclosed. Why this need for secrecy? Has the Gestapo revived? Yes, in another form: the Russian OGPU and the Communist Party. I am shocked. I need not record his story now, sensational as it is—I shall hear it more fully when I get to Berlin.

Luxton invites me to have a meal with him at his club, the Yacht Club. It is on the lake-side opposite to the Atlantic, a smaller and quieter place, large attractive rooms, a good meal, but without ostentatious luxury. Afterwards we sit and talk on the balcony overlooking the lake. It is a beautiful summer evening and hunger and misery seem impossible. The white yachts swerve over the water, and a long rowing-boat, with three girls, bare legs and arms, keeping perfect time, swishes past. "Germans?" I ask. "Good Lord, no!" exclaims Luxton. "The lake is reserved for us."

We sit and talk about Germany, about the British Labour Movement, Socialism, peace and war. "You were among the conchies in the first World War?" he asks. "Yes." "Well, I take off my hat to them. There were some attached to my parachute regiment in this war—R.A.M.C. boys. They were the bravest men I ever met. Entirely unarmed, they dropped from the planes, not knowing where they would fall, perhaps into a nest of Nazis. They went about their job, with firing all about them, fearless and with incredible calm. By God, they were brave !"

I am reluctant to leave, but I want to sort out all the information I've got to-day from the Mil. Gov. high-ups. I return to Warcormess and work at a table in my bedroom, overlooking the garden on which the darkness quietly descends.

THE BRITISH OFFICIAL MIND

Well, what have I learned to-day? One incidental point, yet in the eyes of the high-ups important. As demobilisation proceeds, they are losing their right-hand men. Of the twelve members of the Hamburg Mil. Gov. secretariat, five are going by June. In the Education Section, five are going by August. On the whole, and with certain reservations, I have been impressed by the efficiency of Mil. Gov. staff. Will capable men be sent to replace those who go? I suppose this must be a factor in deciding the level of comfort of the officer class here. They cannot be expected to come unless they have attractive conditions, and yet, to sensitive people, this comfort must be intolerable amidst the prevailing privation. That's a fundamental problem of Occupation.

I've seen into the official mind to-day, the mind which regards the problem of Germany as one of long-term mental and moral re-education. It is looking for "repentance" and sees no sign of it yet. The Communist Party admits the responsibility of the German people for the past. Occasionally a preacher admits it, including the Bishop of Hamburg. But among the people as a whole, in the official view, there is no "change of heart": it will be a long, long task—probably over two generations.

Is it really thought that the Occupation can go on so long? Well, the military mind reassures me: it will not require a large army if the Germans are not allowed any army at all. And why should not our peace-time army be stationed primarily in Germany rather than in Britain? There are thousands of acres of good military exercise ground, and in these days of transport by plane Hanover is little farther away than Salisbury Plain. This view is held quite dispassionately. There is no spirit of revenge in it—indeed, revenge is ruled out. It is a view which is held reluctantly, regretfully.

As I jot down these notes on the official attitude, I want to add comment and criticism. But this is a diary: not a political thesis. At present my task is to report; perhaps later I can retort.

Education. A job seems to have been done here. *Every single child above five years of age in Hamburg is at school.* They go only for half a day, the school buildings are knocked about, the supply of books and equipment is woefully inadequate; but still they go. Probably the best thing about their going is the school-feeding. Twice a week the children get what is called the "Pacific Packet"—rations which were prepared for British troops in the Far Eastern war and which were sent instead to the German children when Japanese resistance collapsed. I'm told the food is not tasty, but it is high in protein and vitamin values. In addition, most of the children get Swedish Red Cross meals four days a week.* Perhaps this is the explanation why so many of them look sturdier than German adults.

The teaching profession has been de-Nazified, yet the schools are short of only 600 teachers in 6,000. This fact hits me: either the de-Nazification has been on a limited scale or the teaching profession was much less Nazi-minded than we have been led to believe. The school-books have all been vetted and new "Readers" and history books are being produced. Our folk are particularly pleased with a new history and with a primer for young children which will shortly be available.

Yesterday afternoon the teacher whom I met at Frau Huth's complained that classical rather than modern education is being introduced for girls. She said that ten hours are spent on Latin and Greek and only two hours on natural science. The official explanation is interesting, but not quite convincing. Under the Nazi régime, girls' education was directed towards preparing them for *Kinder, Küche, Kirche* (Children, Kitchen and Church). The new British régime aims to give the girls as broad an education as the boys. Latin and Greek are necessary for the University entrance examinations. Therefore the considerable time given to them. It is *not* natural science which has been cut down, but *domestic* science. (I must consult the teacher about this. She is not the type which would want girls to be tied down to a kitchen.)

SHOULD "EFFICIENCY" COME FIRST IN AGRICULTURE?

Agriculture. Is it true that more food is being grown in the Russian zone and that rations are higher? Eastern Germany certainly has the richest food production area, but even official

* In June it was announced that the Swedish Red Cross supplies will come to an end in July until the autumn harvest is in.

information about what is happening in the Russian zone seems to be incomplete. The general impression is that food conditions vary greatly: that the chaos in transport means that some areas have less food than in the British zone, whilst some have more. The British have no "golden East", no wide acres of waving corn. All bread must be imported: all available potatoes must be kept for seed. At present the food situation is touch and go. It certainly won't be possible to raise the rations for two or three months.

Efficiency is evidently the first aim of the agricultural organisation. Here's a test. Dr. Schlange-Schöningen has been appointed Agricultural Adviser. Should he have been? Some of the Left are denouncing him as a reactionary, but the official view is that he is the best available expert and that his record proves him a democrat. True he had large estates in Pomerania, but he is stated to have been denounced by the Junkers for his progressiveness. He was a "Progressive-Conservative", elected to the Reichstag in 1923, was in the Bruening Government as Minister without Portfolio in 1928–29, retired from political life when Hitler came to power.

Dr. Schlange-Schöningen typifies the problem which the British face. If the old system is to be retained, the Schlange-Schöningens are probably necessary. But if a new system is to be introduced, breaking with the old economic order of Germany as completely as democracy breaks with Nazism politically, new men will be required.

There I will leave it for to-night. It's getting on for one o'clock.

THE FOURTH DAY

May 1st, 1946.

MAY DAY—the first free May Day in Germany for thirteen years. I am up betimes because at eight the interpreter of my speech—young Heinz Heydorn—is coming to prepare his German translation. He doesn't arrive in fact until nearly nine, because the early trains are so overcrowded that he could not board them. The demonstration is at ten, so Wolf and Heinz have to work at top speed translating and typing.

As our car reaches the city centre we run along by the side of processions, banners stretching across the marching fours, red flags carried singly, bands playing, the people singing—yes, that's The International! As I lean forward to look, I think how like a London procession; and that thought jolts me sharply. I remember pre-Hitler processions in Germany—and my comment had always been how *unlike* British processions. In Britain we cannot march, but in Germany they could, tidy rows of four, swinging in step. They *could*—but this procession isn't. It drags like ours. The explanation comes to me. People cannot march with shoulders back and legs out on 1,000 calories a day.

This is a Trade Union demonstration, and the new German Trade Union movement has made one great advance on the old—it includes all the sections which made chaos of its organisation in the pre-Hitler days. There are no Social Democratic, Christian and Red Trade Unions now. Socialists, Catholics and Communists are joined in the Free Trade Unions. They are demonstrating together to-day.

But, whilst this unity has been secured, the rival working-class parties are still out to prove their strength. The Communists applied for permission to organise their processions. Agreed—starting time 7 a.m. The Social Democrats could not be outdone. Agreed—starting time 8 a.m. This is the end of one of the Social Democratic processions we are overtaking. I read the red slogans on their white banners: "Internationale Zusammenarbeit der Sozialisten!" (International Cooperation of Socialists) and "Für Frieden und Völkerverständigung" (For

Peace and Peoples' Reconciliation). These long German words are a problem for banner designers!

HAMBURG'S MAY DAY DEMONSTRATION

We approach the gates of the park (*Planten un Blomen*). The people crowd the road so that the car cannot move. We get out and are surrounded by excited stewards. It is five minutes to ten, they exclaim, and the broadcast begins at ten. The broadcast? Yes, don't I know?—the meeting and my speech are to be broadcast all over the British zone. As I hear, I marvel once more at British democracy. Without knowing in the least what I am going to say, Mil. Gov. is going to distribute my words to millions of Germans under its occupation!

But I haven't time to think about this. The stewards are rushing Heinz and me through the crowd where it is still thin, along the side of a small lake; it becomes too thick to make headway, and we turn and push to the left until we reach its edge; then we clamber up a hill skirting this vast mass of people, and finally scramble heartless over flower-beds along the top until we reach a platform where a rostrum draped in red has been built in space, like an eagle's nest. Kammeraus, the big transport workers' leader, is addressing the crowd from it. Whilst he is still speaking a man's choir, grouped behind me, begins to sing softly: a background to his words. I turn to look at the choir; the conductor is oldish and so are most of the singers. They must be veterans of the pre-Hitler days—I try to imagine what their emotions must be, singing again freely on this first free May Day. Their voices die away, a new figure is on the rostrum, he is announcing my name.

I step on to the rostrum, am conscious for a moment of a storm of cheering, and then forget everything because of the wonder of the scene before me. I've never in my life seen a crowd like this. It sinks below me down to the distant lake nearly half a mile away and stretches both to left and right. On the further side of the lake is a row of red flags, drooping from their staffs, shimmering in the mirror of the water. I remember that this is the first May Day demonstration since Hitler, that I am the first Britisher to speak to German workers since the war, and temporarily my nerves fail. I am glad that the cheering goes on, giving me a respite; I am glad that, unusually, I have written out my speech. I open with a passage in German, but that is only to explain that my German is not good enough for me to continue. After that, Heinz interprets paragraph by paragraph. To judge from the applause which greets the

44

original sentences, a surprisingly large proportion of the audience understands English. I conclude with Marx's "Workers of all Lands Unite". The cheering is terrific.

During the speech there had been a few minutes' rain. "A happy omen," says a comrade. "Hitler so regularly had rain-less days for his demonstrations that good weather is called 'Hitler weather'!" I remember the ceaseless rain when I left London and remark to myself that 'Hitler weather' is one of the few things we would readily take over. There is one thing which this meeting has taken over which we in Britain would love to possess: the Hitler loudspeaking apparatus. It was one of the prizes captured from the Nazi Labour Front, and I've never heard voices carried so far or so naturally, without any suggestion of the mechanical or blaring ugliness which so often makes our loud-speakers instruments of torture. The Nazis were certainly masters of the technique of mass propaganda.

One unexpected incident happens before I leave. I suddenly see Brigadier Armitage, the Commander of Hamburg, coming towards me with outstretched hand. "I listened to your speech over the wireless," he says, "and as soon as it was over I had to come in my car to congratulate you." I am grateful but be-wildered. My speech was a forthright declaration of inter-national working-class solidarity. It urged that the food supplies of the world should be distributed according to need and that industry should be retained to enable the German people to live and become a part of a co-operative European economy; it included a declaration for workers' and tech-nicians' control as essential to industrial democracy and for common action by the workers of all lands to prevent rulers again sending us to mutual slaughter—*and the Military Com-mander jumps into a car to congratulate me!* Europeans say they cannot understand the ways of the English. I cannot myself. Perhaps we are just incredibly courteous and tolerant.

BANNER WHICH HAS BEEN TWICE BURIED

I learn for the first time now that I am advertised to address another May Day Trade Union demonstration at Harburg, a small industrial town twelve miles away. Heinz and I are taken to a car and we speed away. The demonstration is in an open space in the woods, the platform a gun emplacement. Large Trade Union banners, with old-fashioned woven designs of engines and hammers, are held by veterans on three sides of the emplacement. Beneath it is grouped another men's choir, with a conductor who takes his office very seriously, and then in a

45

large semi-circle stretches the crowd to the edge of the wood. The crowd seems quite small after Hamburg, not more than 3,000.

There is no loud-speaker, and I discard my manuscript. At Hamburg I spoke to a crowd; here I speak with them. We make contact with a close friendliness, and, when I see men crying because of the new hope of Internationalism which the presence of a British Socialist gives, I find it difficult to restrain my own emotion. At the end of the meeting I am mobbed by men and women who want to shake my hand. A sixty-year-old banner-bearer proudly points to its inscription—"Harburg Factory Workers' Union, 1869". It has been hidden under the earth for twelve years during the Bismark anti-labour laws and again for twelve years during the Hitler régime. And here it is waving openly in the wind! It bears the eternal appeal: "Workers of the World, Unite". The conductor of the choir is waiting impatiently at my side. He shows me the sheet of Socialist songs which have been used. They are dated 1904. They, too, have been hidden successfully during the Hitler days.

This is May Day and a general holiday. The children are crowding into the tent of a circus—just about the most human thing I have yet seen in Germany. I have a drink with the local Trade Union leaders at an open-air café. They are proud of the fact that in this small town of 70,000 inhabitants they have enrolled 15,000 Trade Unionists in less than a year. There are not many British towns which can show a higher proportion.

I find Wolf back at the Warcormess before me. He has paid a visit to the Communist Party headquarters in Hamburg and reports that their officials are enthusiastic about my speech. "Something must have been wrong with that speech," I retort. "The Social Democrats were enthusiastic, General Armitage was enthusiastic, the Communists are enthusiastic. I distrust United Fronts as broad as that."

A War Criminal's Last Letter

We have a visitor for dinner, the Prosecutor in a War Criminals' Trial. The verdict is to be given to-morrow and there is no doubt that the sentence will be death. He shows us a letter which a prisoner has written to him, one of the most dignified documents I have ever read. This man, with the certainty of death before him, writes to the Prosecutor acknowledging the fairness of the trial, acknowledging that he authorised the barbarities with which he is charged. He does not wish to justify himself; he wishes to explain. He believed in Nazism; he believed it meant a rebirth for Germany and for the world. He believed in contrast that Bolshevism meant human degradation, that it was accursed. At a critical point in the Russian campaign orders came to him that he must carry through the cold-blooded killings with which he was charged. They were horrible to him; but what was the alternative? To mutiny when the fate of Nazism and Bolshevism hung in the balance? Hating what he did, he obeyed the orders he had received because he felt that course to be the lesser crime. He did not complain of his fate; but he asked that he should be believed when he said that he went through mental torture before deciding and that his decision was made with an honest desire to do what, according to his lights, was right.

The sincerity of this letter was evident. One could not accept his political values. One abhorred the barbarity which he had ordered his men to commit. But that this terrible dilemma had existed for him could not be denied. Such is the logic of totalitarianism, where one has to subordinate one's sense of right and wrong to the will of those who seem masters of men's fate.

I See Starvation Cases in Hospital

I have arranged to go this afternoon to the hospital. The car drives through blossoming orchards to the village of Langenhorn, twelve miles outside Hamburg. The head of the hospital is Dr. Bansi, the greatest nutrition expert in Germany, one of the greatest in the world. Before the war his pre-eminence was recognised by appointment to the Health Commission of the League of Nations.

We turn up a drive, dotted with people visiting patients. The average English hospital is a barrack-like affair: not so this. There are many homely buildings standing amidst grass and gardens. We drive up to the main building, and Dr. Bansi, with two nurses in the background, is standing on the steps to welcome me. He is a little man, clean-shaven, dark, going bald, friendly yet direct and decisive of speech. I'm led into a reception-room and am rather taken aback by the impressive group awaiting me—four or five doctors in white hospital suits and as many sisters and nurses in uniform. I'm introduced and led to a table.

On the table are two trays and a newly-painted cream-coloured tin box. My attention is directed first to the trays. The smaller one is about 30 inches by 18. The larger, about 36 inches by 24. On the former is the total day's ration for the normal adult German citizen. On the latter is the total day's ration for patients in the hospital suffering from physical defects.

47

Honestly, the collection of foodstuffs on the smaller tray would not satisfy the average Englishman for one meal. There are two-and-a-half slices of dry bread, a big potato, fragments of meat and fish, and mere spoonsful of other articles. The tray and its pathetic collection of tit-bits reminds me of the dolls' party games which children play, with tiny morsels of food for their toy tea-sets. I take a note-book from my pocket and write down the exact items as Dr. Bansi recites them. I feel that pen and paper are recording a false impression: the list takes quite a long time to write down and the diet looks varied. I under-line the trifling weights: *they* are what counts. Here is what I wrote:

Bread	.	.	155 grammes (2½ *slices*)
Butter	.	.	11 grammes (*slightly more than ⅓rd oz.*)
Margarine	.	.	2 grammes (*1/16th oz.*)
Cheese	.	.	2 grammes (*1/16th oz.*)
Fresh fish	.	.	32 grammes (*1 oz.*)
Salt fish	.	.	16 grammes (*½ oz.*)
Meat	.	.	25 grammes (*slightly more than ¾ oz.*)
Skimmed milk	.	.	⅛th of a litre (*half a cup*)
Meal	.	.	14 grammes (*less than ½ oz.*)
Soup essence	.	.	14 grammes (*less than ½ oz.*)
Cereals	.	.	35 grammes (*less than 1 1/10th oz.*)
Marmalade	.	.	16 grammes (*½ oz.*)
Potatoes	.	.	286 grammes (*less than 9 oz.*)
Ersatz coffee	.	.	5 grammes (*slightly less than ⅙th oz.*)
Vegetables	.	.	57 grammes (*slightly more than 1¾ oz.*)
Sugar	.	.	18 grammes (*9/16ths oz.*)

This is a day's ration *on paper*. In fact, many of its items are often unobtainable. Potatoes, for example, haven't been pro-curable for months. When this happens, other items are increased or substitutes given. As I have already found, hard turnips, which would ordinarily be given to cattle, are the staple food in most homes.

On the second tray the rations are larger. For example, there are 4¼ slices of dark bread instead of 2½. The calorie value of the diet for physical cases is about one-third higher than for adults outside.

The Scientific Facts About Hunger

Dr. Bansi begins to talk and the doctors and nurses group themselves round us to listen. He gives me in fifteen minutes more *facts* about the food situation than I've got from all the other people I've consulted. I don't think I have yet put down the scale of daily rations in the British zone. Here they are:

Basic	.	.	.	1,048 calories
Heavy workers	.	.	.	1,753 calories
Very Heavy workers	.	.	2,312 calories
British civilians	.	.	2,800 calories

The 2,800 calories allowed to British civilians represents the normal ration which we have at home. It is between two and three times as much as the basic ration of the German people. The rations of Britishers in the Forces and the Control Commission in Germany are much higher.

The next striking fact worthy of record is this. *The rations of the Nazi prisoners in the internment camps is considerably higher than the rations of ordinary German civilians.* This is not because the British authorities love the Nazis, but because they found that the disease and death-rate threatened to become so alarming on the usual ration that they simply had to increase it. Here are the figures for the Nazi prisoners:

Non-workers	.	.	.	1,250 calories
Workers	.	.	.	1,600 calories
Ill	.	.	.	1,700 calories

These calorie values are still terribly low, but I note that *non-working* Nazi internees get one-fifth more than workers on lighter jobs outside the prison camps.

Dr. Bansi hesitates a moment. "I could cite so much evidence of the increasing starvation," he remarks, "that I don't know what to select." He begins to pour out facts, whilst I jot them down in my note-book. As I listen and write, I wish my journalist colleagues at the Warcormess were with me: if they were here, they *couldn't* belittle Germany's hunger. I tabulate the main evidence:

Mortality of Babies in Hamburg.

1939	.	.	58·06 per thousand
1943	.	.	57·98 per thousand
1944	.	.	97·40 per thousand
1945	.	.	134·15 per thousand

Why this huge increase in 1945? Partly it will have been due to the first cuts in rations at the end of the war, but are deaths from bombing also included? Dr. Bansi rushes on before I have time to ask. But there was no bombing in 1946, and the figures

49

which the doctor is now giving are still very high. He takes the
first four months of this year separately:

1946	1st week to 4th week	.	.	.	112·6 per thousand.
	5th week to 8th week	.	.	.	98·0 per thousand.
	9th week to 12th week	.	.	.	105·7 per thousand.

In April came the last severe cut in rations. This is what it
meant in the loss of infants' lives:

   13*th week to* 16*th week* . . . 184·2 *per thousand*

Such are the figures. I hold my pen for a moment and try to
think of the mothers and their children: more than one in six
of the babies dying.

The next set of figures Dr. Bansi gives me relate to school-
children. I take them down before thinking about their
significance:

Nutrition and Health of 10,000 *School-children in Hamburg.*

Period.	Bad.	Medium.	Good.
1945 September to December .	*32·7	36·9	30·4
1946 March 18 to 23 . .	39·2	38·8	22·0
March 25 to 30 . .	44·9	41·3	14·0
April 1 to 6 . . .	45·5	36·2	18·3
April 8 to 13 . . .	63·6	20·5	15·3

That heavy jump of "bad" in the second week of April—what
can it mean except the effect of the last ration cut? Look at
it—the nutrition and health of more than three out of five
school-children are *bad!*

Dr. Bansi gives me some evidence of weights. He cites the
weights of patients in a large hospital, Eppendorfer Hospital,
where they have been recorded systematically since 1939. In
that year 22·4 per cent of the patients were under-weight and
31·1 per cent over-weight. *Now* 54·4 *per cent are under-weight and*
5·8 *over-weight.* Since 1945 the under-weights have increased by
9·7 per cent and the over-weights have fallen by 4·3 per cent.
The percentage of "under-weights" among the sick is, of
course, greater than among the ordinary population: it is the
huge *increase* in the percentage which is significant. When I
ask Dr. Bansi if he has evidence of the under-weight frequency
in the general community, he refers to sample weighings made
in the streets of Hamburg at the end of April, 1946. *Twenty-
one per cent* were below normal weight.

Hospitals everywhere report that malnutrition cases are

growing steadily, says the doctor. "The whole population in the British zone receive such a small ration that each individual is like an engine which is burning not only fuel but its own body," he explains. "They cannot live and work on the food which they eat, so they are living and working on the reserve of energy which is in their muscles. *It is a kind of cannibalism.* They are living and working by eating themselves."

Food Elements From Human Hair

He describes how he and his colleagues at the hospital have proved this by a careful investigation of the "intake" (food consumed) and the "output" (urine and excreta) of the patients. I cannot follow all this, but I do understand that they have been able to itemise the elements which are lacking for the maintenance of health. Some of these elements are present in yeast, which they have been able to obtain from wood, but yeast is still without the necessary amino-acids. "We need cystins," proceeds Dr. Bansi. "This is how we get it to enable the malnutrition cases in this hospital to recover." He stretches his hand across the table and places the newly-painted cream-coloured tin box in front of me. He raises its lid—*and it is full of human hair!*

I gasp, and look again into the box. The contents are beautifully clean and soft, but there is no doubt that what I see is human hair. I look into Dr. Bansi's face. "You are getting this necessary food element from human hair?" I exclaim.

"Yes. Our researches at the Hamburg Chemical Institute have shown how cystins can be extracted from it. We are now collecting all the hair from our patients when it is cut, immunising it, and extracting the food element which is lacking. The patients then at it mixed in their foods. You shall eat some for yourself."

"Is this being done anywhere else in the world?"

"Not so far as we know. We have only just begun it. The results have proved so satisfactory that we are now making arrangements to collect hair from all the barbers in Hamburg."

I am stunned into silence. There is something that revolts me in the idea that human beings should be fed on human hair. It's in the nature of the cannibalism which Dr. Bansi has already instanced. But, I reflect, it is better that human beings should be fed on their discarded hair than on their living muscles. . . . My thoughts are interrupted by a movement in the group of doctors and nurses who surround me. "Let us pass on to the malnutrition ward," Dr. Bansi is saying.

51

There are forty-two cases. I cannot describe them. I look from one bed to another and want to look away. Faces yellow and grey, foreheads and cheeks streaked with deep furrows, eyes which show the fear and pain and exhaustion which have been undergone. I try to recollect where I have seen such faces before. It was in the film of the Belsen camp. . . . Thank God Dr. Bansi is talking. It distracts my attention from this horror. He is saying that when the malnutrition cases come into the hospital their weights have gone up: that surprises me. I look at these ugly human forms again and, at his direction, feel the bodies with my hands. They are puffed out with water. I press my fingers on their legs: it is like pressing a half-sucked orange —the dent remains in the squashy flesh until the water gradually fills it up. Two nurses lift a sheet: Dr. Bansi slaps the thigh of a patient and invites me to do so. The thigh is like a hot water-bottle, with the water gone luke-warm.

These patients are suffering from malnutrition dropsy. When the water has been drawn from the bodies, the skin hangs on the bones as though there were no flesh, no fat, no muscles— just skeletons covered by crinkled skin. Cannibalism is the right word. These humans have lived on themselves until there is nothing but bone and skin left. The water extracted, the weight falls with a bang. Then comes the difficult task of building up their bodies on a diet which is below human need, building up the flesh and the muscle from yeast drawn from wood and from cystins extracted from human hair.

The earlier patients here were returned prisoners-of-war from Poland and France and internees from Nazi concentration camps. They have sufficiently recovered to be walking about, and I talk with them, wondering what it is beyond the firmness of their limbs and cheeks which distinguishes them: then I realise—they are smiling, the distraught expression has gone. Their clothes still hang loosely on them, but Dr. Bansi has performed the miracle of recovery with less than allows for normal strength.

The later patients are starvation cases from the ordinary German population: most of them have come in recently and the entries are increasing each week. The cases are practically all old or single men living alone. When one lives in a family, a younger doctor remarks, opportunities are found to make the best of the collective ration or to supplement it: one or more of the home circle brings extras in from the country or does a deal in the black market. It is the lonely men who suffer. Dr. Bansi emphasises that the forty-two cases in this male ward by no means represent the "hunger" patients in the hospital. These are the simple "malnutrition" cases—men suffering from starvation without other complications. But hunger stimulates other diseases, particularly tuberculosis, and all these diseases are going up. Moreover, the starved condition of the body makes it far more difficult to resist the attack of the disease. The death-rate of all the diseases is going up alarmingly.

As I leave the ward a nurse approaches with a plate on which there are fingers of toast covered with a brown paste. "Taste our special food preparation," invites Dr. Bansi. "Including the cystins from human hair?" I ask. "Yes," he replies. I am a vegetarian, but I am too intrigued to decline. The doctors and nurses watch me with interest as I bite and swallow. "Not bad," I comment. The taste is not unlike fish-paste.

MENTAL PATIENTS ON THE "HITLER DIET"

We cross gardens to another building. "I want you to see the mental patients," says Dr. Bansi. They are grouped in a living-room around two tables. Some of them stand as we enter, making a tableau. It is the most ghastly tableau I have ever seen. I cannot glance at these men and women a second time: I turn and have gone in thirty seconds. The face of one of the women will haunt me as long as I live: a young woman, little more than thirty, but with the suffering of ages in her eyes. It is not madness which horrifies me in these faces, but hunger. White, hollow faces with a pain and appeal in their eyes which are unbearable.

I cannot speak for a time and I do not hear what Dr. Bansi is saying. Then I pick it up. These mental patients do not get the extra ration allowed to the physical cases. They were deliberately starved under Hitler; they are starving now under the British Occupation. It was found that Nazi prisoners could not exist on the 1,048 calorie ration and it was increased; but these prisoners of the mind are still left to the torture of existing on it. They never have anything beyond it: no one ever brings them anything from the country or a prize from the black market or scraps from the tables or dustbins of the British. They go all round the hours hungry, until a merciful death ends their physical and mental pain. A lethal chamber would be humane compared with this ordeal.*

* When I returned to London I drew Mr. John Hynd's attention to this barbarity. He replied that the original instruction to increase rations in hospitals had been misunderstood. Because asylums were not specifically mentioned, the increases had not been given to mental patients. He had sent

I have only an indistinct memory of saying good-bye to Dr. Bansi and his colleagues. I am so shaken that I feel nothing except an utter exhaustion. The car rushes me back to Hamburg. I have to speak at the May Day meeting of the Social Democratic Party in Broadcasting House, and I must somehow put out of my mind what I have seen. I try to jot down a few notes for my speech, but not successfully. When I get to the hall the meeting has begun and I am guided into a seat against the wall on the ground floor. An orchestra of fifty instrumentalists is playing the Triumphal March from "Aïda" and everyone is listening intently. From this side seat I can look at the hall and the people without turning about or disturbing anyone. It is a beautiful hall, light and spacious, with three narrow galleries on either side, running into a deep, ascending gallery at the back. The people don't look as though they have come to a political meeting: they are wrapt in the music as completely as an Albert Hall audience at a symphony concert. There is a large proportion of young people among them, larger than at this morning's Trade Union demonstrations. I am still worried about the speech. I jot down some heads, but am not satisfied. . . . I listen to the music. The orchestra is playing Rossini's William Tell overture. I am not tutored in music, but I find it beautiful and the strain of mind and emotion begins to ease. The piece ends and the audience bursts into applause. I whip out the piece of paper with my notes, strike them out with a pencil, and sketch out a completely different speech on the other side. At last I am satisfied.

The orchestra play for half-an-hour. Then—how memories of German Socialist meetings in the old days revive!—a Speaking Choir. My English friends are sceptical about Speaking Choirs, and I've certainly suffered under crude imitations of them in London. But as I heard them at the Max Rheinhardt Theatre in Berlin before the Nazi days, and as I hear this Choir to-day, I am impressed by their dramatic effect. Thirty or forty actors, workers in overalls, housewives, soldiers, come on to the stage, and one here, one there, utters the misery which is in the hearts of the people. Their heads are bent dejectedly. And then an interruption which we should regard in England as theatrical and which, for a few minutes, I fear will fail here—Karl Meitmann steps into the centre of the stage, the actors grouped about him, and delivers his May Day oration.

---

a new instruction requiring that the increase be immediately extended to mental patients.

54

Can acting and reality mix? My fear is unfounded. After a few sentences, the passionate sincerity of Meitmann and the quality of his diction so win our attention that we forget the other figures, and we are captured by his appeal to turn depression into hope by will and work. He ends and withdraws behind the half-circle of thick red curtains at the back, and we hear the members of the Speaking Choir again. They have caught the spirit of Meitmann's appeal. They express courage and hope. Heads are lifted. They march off the stage in swinging steps of determination to enter the fight.

We have more music—and my turn has come. I speak of the double struggle in which democratic Socialists are engaged— the struggle against Capitalism and the struggle for a Socialism which is libertarian. I am amazed by the response. This morning I was moved by the reception, but it had nothing of the fervour which is here. When I end with *"Freundschaft—Freiheit —Auf Wiedersehen"*, the whole audience shouts the words in unison after me. There is music once more, Greek dancing, reciting and everyone stands to sing the final Socialist song— *"Wann Wir Schreiten Seit' an Seit' "*. Meitmann leads me on to the stage and we sing side by side. Then he takes both my hands and pledges the solidarity of the German and British workers whilst the audience cheer and wave their hands in a tumult of enthusiasm. When we get behind the red curtains again, tears are running down Meitmann's cheeks. "This is the moment I have lived for during twelve years," he exclaims. To an Englishman this may seem undisciplined emotionalism; but remember that this is the first Free May Day in Germany since 1933, remember the isolation which German Socialists still feel, remember that this is the first time that a Socialist from another land has spoken to them as a comrade—and their emotion will be understood.

AN EVENING WITH STUDENTS

Wolf and I return to Warcormess for a meal and then we have a quiet evening's discussion with a few of the leaders of the Socialist Youth in the flat of their chairman. Heinz is there and Grete and Jack Meitmann. They tell me the amusing story of the beginning of the Socialist Students' Association. Two students—one the son of a Social Democratic Party official and another from the Baltic—constitute themselves as the Association and, without asking anyone's permission, put up posters on the University Board calling the first meeting. It was attended by seven persons. Mil. Gov. has prohibited political

Youth Movements,* but still it goes on. The Association has run a series of lectures on such subjects as Socialism and Education, Art and Ethics (as well as on more factual subjects like the Co-operative Movement), and there has been an attendance of from thirty to forty.

University students are still largely Nazi. We are told that probably the majority of the students at Hamburg University are against democracy, though a large number are bewildered and their opinions unformed. There has been some controversy as to whether ex-members of the Hitler Youth should be admitted to the Socialist Youth Movement. The view of the young Germans at our discussion is that not only should they be admitted, a definite effort should be made to convert and enrol them. Most of the Young Nazis never had an opportunity to learn any other philosophy, and the enthusiasm with which many of them served the cause of Nazism is wanted in the completely new Movement of Socialist Youth which has now to be built.

One interesting point emerges from this talk. These young students all insist that if Socialism is to appeal to Youth it must be re-stated in ethical and humanist terms: a new religion. The materialist philosophy of the old Marxism cannot re-inspire the new generation in Germany. If their mental and spiritual void is to be filled, it must be by a faith which supplies a new moral code, a new reverence for human personality, a new sense of human values, a new human solidarity which extends to all peoples. They are so united in this view that I ask them whether they have come under the influence of any particular teacher. No, they have discussed the subject among themselves, but their conviction is based mostly on their knowledge of the mental and spiritual hunger of their fellow-students and on their experience when seeking to satisfy it.

This is probably the most significant thing we have heard in Germany so far. Wolf and I discuss it in the car returning to Warcormess. At times of great disaster there is always a tendency to turn to religion as an escape from reality. These students want a religion which is attached to reality. This may be their contribution not only to German Socialism, but finally to the Socialist Movement of the world.

* I raised this matter with Mr. John Hynd on my return to London and he tells me the ban has now been withdrawn.

one farthing each in British money—the only souvenirs we can purchase in Hamburg! Along the farther wall we come across what used to be a snack-bar and at last we find some food on sale: a little circle of *erstaz* blancmange, two inches in diameter, surrounded by some thin red *ersatz* jam. *Ersatz* coffee is also on sale. A workman is making his mid-day meal on this; he has of course to surrender coupons for it.

We walk along a street which has seventeen shops in succession without an article in their windows. I have not realised before the colour which the contents of shops give to streets—the brightly covered tins, the fruits, the sweets, the dresses. We complain of their scarcity in Britain. In Hamburg they don't exist.

TRAVELLING TO BERLIN

We travel to Hanover in a *Volkswagon*, Hitler's mass-produced "Ford". An officer sits beside the driver; Wolf and I behind. We start on the autobahn, the first time I have travelled on one of these four-track concrete roads by which Hitler linked the main cities of Germany to Berlin. We have uncomfortable evidence that R.A.F. bombing has been accurate: crossing one of the repaired surfaces my head hits the car-top so that I am nearly stunned. Every bridge has been destroyed (by the Germans) and temporarily repaired (by the British). We take a secondary road to Hanover and travel through delightful woodland country. Beside the road, under the shade of trees, is a grassy track, a godsend to hikers. We pass some lovely little towns, including Bergen, nearby the Belsen camp. I hear that there are 8,000 Jews still in Belsen: they have nowhere to go.

One feature of the little towns impresses immediately. These people are not hungry. There are no grey or yellow haggard faces. The cheeks are full and there is colour in the skin—a healthy, glowing red-brown. The very walking of the people is different. I have never noticed such a contrast between peoples before, perhaps because I learned in Hamburg to observe closely. There is no need to tell us that the countryside is living above the ration level.

As we travel Wolf and I exchange impressions. We have been seeing different things and different people. I tell him of the view I had heard from a Mil. Gov. high-up that there is no "repentance" among the German people. Wolf has been seeking out old friends in Hamburg and has been able to talk to them and their neighbours intimately. They assure him that they had no knowledge of the worse things which were done in the concentration camps: the mass-murders were not referred to in the Nazi press, and when they heard of the B.B.C. broadcasts they not unnaturally thought it was "propaganda". They report that a feeling of sympathy with the Jews and the conscripted foreign workers was widespread and that a surprising number of Germans risked Gestapo persecution by helping them. Among non-political Germans there is a feeling that they were not responsible for what happened: it had been done by Hitler, and Hitler's power was so great that the ordinary man in the street could not influence events. If the point is put to them that they should not have allowed Hitler to get such power, they agree in the light of subsequent events—the war, the Nazi infamies and the disaster which has come to Germany —but in the beginning Hitler gave them work and security which they had not known before, and they did not realise its consequences. They are now disillusioned, but in the Nazi days they had no means of understanding.

My contribution to this discussion is the impression that German Social Democrats are often reacting unhealthily to the charge of guilt. They have developed an inferiority complex; they are servile to Mil. Gov.; there is an absence of self-reliance and independence. The healthy reaction would have been a zeal for democracy so great that it would challenge the principle of dictatorship wherever it showed itself, whether in the ranks of German reaction or in the Occupation Powers; a passion for equality so great that it would challenge every obstruction to the creation of a unified Socialist Germany and to the incorporation of that Germany in a united Socialist Europe. That is not yet the spirit of German Social Democracy as I have seen it.

Wolf agrees, and adds that he had found Communist Party initiative and competence much greater than among the Social Democrats. He visited the K.P.D. and S.P.D. headquarters in Hamburg and found the technical standard of the former much higher than the latter: both the ability and the size of staff and equipment. He was impressed with the speed and thoroughness of the information which he got from the Communists compared with the sketchy vagueness of the Social Democrats. Part of this efficiency is no doubt due to the help in paper supplies and office set-up obtained from the Russians, but it is not only this. The Communists here, as nearly everywhere, work with an enthusiasm and efficiency above those of their rival parties.

At the same time Wolf has come to one clear conclusion: the hope of free and democratic Socialism lies in the Social Democratic Party. In pre-Hitler days he had been as a youth in the Communist Party and then one of the Communist Opposition groups. A number of the C.O.s have now rejoined the Communist Party; many have not. Wolf is among the latter, because he cannot accept its trend towards dictatorial collectivism or its treatment of other sections of the working-class. He has no doubt at all that it is the duty of German Socialists to enter enthusiastically into the Social Democratic Party, which he now regards as the only instrument for the realisation of a free Socialist Germany.

I am more aware of the British Occupation on this journey than I have yet been. The Transport Section of Mil. Gov. has certainly taken possession of the roads. Every hundred yards or so there are large, clear notices telling the British driver all he can possibly want to know: any stranger could reach his destination mapless and without knowing a word of German. Our driver is a German, but he keeps his eyes on the British signs and acknowledges they are the best he has ever seen.

First Visit to Hanover

We arrive in the "posh" area of Hanover—impressive, almost castle-like houses in grey stone. They have been knocked about more than the residences of the wealthy of Hamburg, perhaps because the industrial and "select" districts are less distant here. As we approach the railway station I am surprised to see hundreds of people camped in the square which fronts it: whole families sitting around their baggage, with apparently no early prospects of trains. In the station itself the passages are crowded with similar groups: I had read of this in Russia, but have never seen it. I am told that these people are trekking east and west. Some are emigrating from eastern parts of Germany, where they have been turned out by Russians, Poles and Czechs: others are trekking back to eastern Germany, hoping that they may get settled in their home territories again. I learn the significant news that the west–east trek is now becoming stronger than the east–west trek. Why? Because there is more food in the Russian zone and the early chaos is being replaced by some semblance of order.

I want to go to the cloakroom in the station. The passage is blocked by two armed soldiers. One of them orders me to go by a roundabout route, traversing stairs, platforms and bridges. The voice is Scottish. "Do you know Jimmie Maxton?" I ask. "Who doesn't?" the soldier replies. "He's a friend of mine," I say. "Go right through," he instructs, stepping aside. Meanwhile, I have lost Wolf. I find him on the edge of a group of Germans, with a railway foreman shouting angrily at him. He is being denounced because he is in British uniform. I had expected this to happen before: what should we think at home if a Britisher walked our streets in German uniform? The shouting stops as I approach, but I feel sorry for Wolf. He is a German Socialist, and to him a British uniform must be even more irksome than it is to me.

There is no train to Berlin until nearly midnight. We drive out to the Officers' Transit Camp, in a barracks in the suburbs of Hanover, for a meal. Dinner is over, but it is served for us specially and plentifully, in a huge empty mess-room. Afterwards we sit in a lounge, where men and women officers sit in easy-chairs chatting over drinks from the cocktail bar.

At eleven our transport is ready to take us to a station. It consists of a covered truck, dimly lit, with wooden forms on either side: we couldn't be travelling harder if we were refugees or prisoners. Two German boys are in charge: two German girls come out to them (I suspect they hand the boys some left-over food), and the four talk and laugh regardless of us or the six British officers who climb in with us. I can't help being amused. This is the first time I've been physically uncomfortable in Germany or seen British officers uncomfortable. It's the first time I've been in the presence of Germans who are obviously happier and more care-free than we are. The incident is trivial and passing; yet it stands out vividly in my memory.

THROUGH THE RUSSIAN ZONE

At the station the platform is crowded, but our sense of "privilege" is restored when we climb into a first-class carriage and stretch our legs the length of the seats. A soldier comes to the door. "I've a sleeper for two," he says. "Would you like it?" He sees the labels on our uniforms. "Newspaper men? Then I should advise you to sit up and keep awake. We sometimes have fun on this train." We are interested. "We pass through the Russian zone," he explains, "and now and again they search us to make sure there are no civilians on board. Wouldn't that make a good story?" "We'll wake up quickly enough if that happens," I retort. "We'll take the sleeper."

THE SIXTH DAY

May 3rd, 1946.

WHEN I awake, Wolf is already dressed and standing at the window. We are nearing his home ground, from which he has been exiled for ten years. The train rattles through Potsdam station. Wolf whistles. The town is down, not bombed (he thinks), but shelled into a wilderness. We approach Berlin's outskirts. He goes on whistling. These districts are destroyed beyond recognition, except for the station names. I dress. Wolf tells me that since we entered the Russian zone there has been only one railway track. "The other has been dismantled and the steel taken to Russia," he remarks.

Both of us knew Charlottenburg station in the old days, but we don't know it now. The whole structure has gone, the platform and rails alone remaining. When driving, however, to the Berlin Warcormess, located at Berlin's Savoy, the *Hotel Am Zoo*, we do not see more damage than one sees in central parts of London. The Kurfürstendamm is also more like West End London than anything we have seen in Hamburg. There are concert-halls, cinemas, cafés—and shops!*

My room at the hotel is on the second floor, a long, neatly-furnished room with bed, basin with running water, settee, table, wardrobe, desk, an arm-chair and a straight chair. What more would you? In the hotel restaurant breakfast is served by professional waiters. I remark that the crockery is like the silver-grey sets we use at home, but thicker. Wolf looks at the bottom of his cup and finds a swastika design with the motto "Beauty of Work" round it. How the Nazis sloganised and idealised everything!

Twenty or so War Correspondents—British, French, Dutch, Norwegian—are at other tables, with a dozen Mil. Gov. officers belonging to the Public Relations Section. We have our customarily good breakfast. Afterwards, we go to the 5 P.R.S. office on a higher floor and get, among other things, passes into

---

* Later we find that, despite a brave showing, the contents of the shops are very limited: either old stocks or second-hand goods. The prices are terrific—far beyond the reach of the ordinary person. There are, of course, no foodstuffs outside the ration.

the Russian sector, typed in picturesque but unreadable letters. "I wonder what they've said about us?" I joke to Wolf. "Do you think it's safe to use them?"

We tell the clerk at the reception desk that we want to go to the Control Commission headquarters, and in a flash a car is at the door. The streets are full. "Wolf," I say slowly, "these people are not so hungry as the Hamburg folk." We observe them for a time: the grey, haggard faces are noticeably less frequent. "You're right," says Wolf. I am puzzled by this evidence of greater well-being, because the country is farther off here and food more difficult to scrounge.

The British H.Q. in Germany

Lancaster House, the H.Q. of British administration in Germany, is an impressive building, standing in a circle round a large courtyard. A perpetually moving lift, giving one just time to get in or out at each floor, carries us to the office of the Public Relations Officer, a radiant young man who has "the playing-fields of England" written all over him. He undertakes to fix the interviews we want. At eleven Sir Brian Robertson, second in command in Germany, is holding a Press Conference. Would we like to attend? I would.

Wolf is eager to hunt up comrades. One of them, the woman-head of the Social Democratic educational administration in Berlin in the pre-Hitler days, lives nearby. There is half-an-hour before the Press Conference, so I accompany him.

The work of clearing up the war damage seems to be going on with much greater activity here than in Hamburg. Before the larger wreckage sites, trucks carry the rubble along temporarily laid rails to waiting wagons. I am surprised to see that the work is being done almost entirely by women, young women in their late 'teens and women who must be fifty or sixty. Wolf thinks this may be forced labour by Nazis and we approach a group to enquire. A woman answers my first question in perfect English: a prim little woman of about forty, with black hair drawn tightly back and wearing glasses—the managing type. She is a social worker; but why is she doing this work? Her husband is too ill to earn and her son has T.B., she tells us. She has to get more food, somehow, and she's doing demolition work because it is classed as heavier work and earns higher rations. "How many calories do you get?" asks Wolf. "Two thousand a day," she replies. The figure astonishes me—and then comes the explanation of the healthier appearance of the people here. The ration in all sectors of Berlin is one-third higher than in the British zone. Even so, these women say they become exhausted at their work because of want of food. There is some discussion among them as to whether the work is forced or free. The social worker says she volunteered to do it; another woman says she was directed to it. They work forty-eight hours a week for ¾ marks an hour—that is, 4½d.

A little farther along the road we see some more women on a strange job—they are unloading furniture from a barrow into a cellar under a shattered building. All they have for a home. Then something happens which challenges my view that the Berlin people are not so near hunger. Just as we are passing, an old man totters on the pavement. I throw out my hand and hold him up. He apologises and assures us he'll soon be all right. I guide him to railings and he leans against them. We ask him whether we can take him home. "Oh, no," he says, "it soon passes. I'll walk on quietly in a minute." "Have you been to a doctor?" "Yes. He says he can't do anything. It's want of food."

I leave Wolf to look up the educationalist, making him promise to fix an appointment for me if he finds her. I want to get the facts about the Berlin rations: there is just time to enquire from the Public Relations Officer before going to the Press Conference. I find it is true they are a third higher than in Hamburg. These are the figures:

Basic	1,504 calories
Employees . . .	1,581 calories
Group II workers . .	1,957 calories
Heavy workers . . .	2,443 calories

I also get the figures for children:

To 6 years . . .	1,375 calories
From 6 to 9 . . .	1,473 calories
From 9 to 14 . . .	1,543 calories

These are the rations for all four sectors of Berlin, agreed upon by the British, American, Russian and French authorities. It shows how much I have become conditioned by the Hamburg figures that at first I regard these rations as good. Then I remember that 2,500 calories are the minimum to sustain health. Not even the heavy workers get that! I realise that even with their one-third up Berlin rations are far below the human-need line.

The Press Conference is held in a long room, with a main table seating forty-two persons and two smaller tables seating fifteen more. In front of each seat are pads of paper, a sharpened pencil, and a stencilled memo. Two women shorthand writers, in Mil. Gov. uniform, take their seats at the centre of the large table opposite vacant seats left for Sir Brian Robertson and his staff. Nearly all the other seats are filled by journalists, of many different nationalities, three women among them. Whilst waiting for the Deputy Military Governor (he is said to be the real directing brain) I look at the memo. It is a detailed description of the arrangements planned for the local elections in October.

Sir Brian and a staff of five senior officers enter. They walk in so impressively that I wonder if my fellow-journalists will stand, but no, though in uniform, they are not so regimented as that. My first descriptive note about the Deputy Governor is "distant and superior"; he certainly is that compared with the general on his right hand, a large-built man and, to judge by his geniality, large-hearted. Sir Brian is like a statue, both of figure and face, clean-cut and impassive. Twice during the proceedings his voice is interrupted by a carpenter's knocking. The first time he pauses and frowns, and immediately an officer goes to stop the noise. The second time he says sharply, "Why can't I have silence?"—and the officer is out of the room in a flash, ready for a "kill".

The Deputy Governor soon reveals he has other capacities than disciplinarian. I am lost in admiration of the technical ability with which he presents his case. This military man has the precision, the vocabulary, the clarity and the voice-control of the ablest politician or lawyer. I certainly do not know a Cabinet Minister who speaks more commandingly, knowing his facts, knowing his mind. In turn he discusses food, coal, the transference of functions to Germans, the coming local elections, the change-over from military to civilian personnel—all with the same assurance. Only once does he read from a manuscript. When he does this I feel he is letting us down—just as I feel when Len Hutton bats disappointingly at cricket.

But I am letting my subject down. Whether we have an artist in speech at the head of the British administration in Germany matters little. What matters is that we should have a man of the right attitude of mind and of constructive ability. I do not know Sir Brian's politics; he is probably far from being an International Socialist, certainly no International Socialist can be satisfied with the policy of the British Occupation. But within the limits of his subjects to-day he is good. No one could speak more gravely than he does on food (it is a misfortune that I'm not allowed to quote him). As I listen, I wish those Hamburg journalists who belittle the hunger in Germany were present.

When question time comes, the Deputy Governor proves that he can stall as well as any Cabinet Minister—or stonewall as well as Len Hutton. The most direct and persistent questioner is the representative of the *Manchester Guardian*. In the best Liberal tradition, he wants the discussions at the Allied Control Commission here to be as public as at the Security Council of UNO. Why shouldn't the peoples of the world know the truth about the scarcely-veiled conflict between Russia and the Western Allies? Why aren't food supplies from all zones being pooled? Why is the political and economic unity of Germany being held up? It would be much better to have it out in the open.

The Press Conference over, I am held up by a young woman on the staff. "You represent Left-Wing papers, don't you?" she challenges. "Well, I can give you the low-down about this set-up. They say its being civilianised. The fact is that we civilians are being militarised." She is explosive, and I expect the doors along the passage to be opened by irate officials demanding what the noise is about. This subject is beyond my plan of investigation, but it is interesting. I make a date at her NAAFI for the next night.

What British "Other Ranks" Think

While I wait for the car, I ask a soldier for *his* views on the "set-up". He also is ready to be explosive, but he's on duty and has to restrain himself. He has no doubts: it is the "other ranks" in the Forces who are getting the raw deal. They are paid less than the Control Commission personnel: can anyone blame them for selling cigarettes on the black market when they are not paid enough to live reasonably? His other grounds of complaint are two. First, the distinction between the life of the officer class and of the "other ranks". The officers, he says, are living like gods—the best hotels, cars, night clubs. The "other ranks" are living in barracks or crowded billets; they travel in packed tram-cars; and most of the amusement places are out of bounds. "Gentlemen and floor-wipers" is his description of the two classes. "Thought we won this war for democracy!" he exclaims. "There's more class snobbery in

67

the army now than there was during the war." The other thing that gets him down is the sterner discipline and the insistence on army routine. This he avers is stiffer than during the war, and "all such blasted waste of time, imposed just to get us down and keep us down." I ask him about the civilian girls, whose fiery spokesman I have just met. For them he hasn't much sympathy, mostly on the ground that they can get wines and spirits not available to the "other ranks". He is bitter about the restrictions on amusement. The U.S. soldiers are allowed to go to all places except those marked "out of bounds". British soldiers are allowed to go only to a limited number of places marked "in bounds". There seems to be a widespread revolt against this. In one month a thousand British Tommies were arrested for breaking this regulation. Their pay was stopped for a week. "Depend upon it," he insists, "it's the other ranks in the Forces who are getting the raw deal."

A Berlin Socialist is waiting for me outside the *Hotel Am Zoo* when I return for lunch. I tell him I want to see Socialists in the Russian sector. He advises against for reasons that startle me. "*You* would probably be all right," he says, "but the men whom you visit will become marked men." (How shockingly like the Gestapo this sounds!) He can arrange, however, for four comrades from the Russian sector to meet me on this side of the "frontier". He takes this conspiratorial planning as a matter of course; he became accustomed to it in the underground during the Hitler days and afterwards in a concentration camp. I fix an appointment for to-night.

After lunch I go back to Lancaster House to see the Political heads—first Major Lancashire and then an old acquaintance, Austen Albu, Fabian, member of the influential Clarity Group during the last years of the war. Both are "intellectuals". The Major looks it—the ascetic, philosophic type, but he shows he has much shrewdness. Albu doesn't look an ascetic. He is physically one of the biggest men I've ever met, dominating everyone and everything about him by his huge figure, his gestures, his voice, his laughter, his confidence. He is evidently enjoying his job as Political Adviser to the Military Governor.

Talks with the Berlin "High-Ups"

The car takes me to the Mil. Gov. H.Q. for the British sector of Berlin. It is near the exhibition grounds, and it is curious to see *Der Funkturm* standing erect and high like the Eiffel Tower, as though cocking a snook at the fate which has levelled other buildings.* I spend the afternoon interviewing a series of high-ups, but I won't attempt to describe these talks. The truth is I am too tired to note personal impressions keenly and, in any case, I am not allowed to identify what I hear with individuals. I tell Dr. Melvin, head of the Public Health Department, a genial, free-speaking Scotsman, of Dr. Bansi's experiment with human hair, and he shows great interest, taking notes so that he can follow up with enquiries. There is one part of our conversation I can report. I ask him about malnutrition, the memory of that Hamburg hospital ward still in my mind. He says there is evidence of malnutrition in every hospital and in every street, and then gives me permission to quote from his latest report, which is just being typed by a German girl in the next room. It shows how the death rate from nearly every disease is going up because the patients have lost their resistance power through malnutrition. I take down the figures for dysentery. In March there were fifty-three cases in the British sector of Berlin, of which eleven died. In April the number of cases had fallen to forty-two, but the number of deaths had risen to seventeen.† I fill pages of my note-book with information from my interviews. Let me summarise some of the interesting points.

Education: The difficulty with the staff is not so much Nazi-minded teachers as the prevalence of the old "Prussian" type.

Industry: Stocks of raw materials are exhausted and future supplies are doubtful. This applies particularly to textiles and footwear. Building materials are limited almost entirely to what is rescued from salvage. There is at present no serious unemployment.

De-Nazification: This is working out well because responsibility has been placed on the Germans. The greatest difficulty is with the professions. For example, there is hardly a politically reliable doctor in Berlin. (Why not send for those Socialist doctors in Hamburg?)

Health: Considering the appalling state of the city after the Battle of Berlin, the check on disease has been remarkable. There has been no outbreak of epidemics, as might have been feared. In the early months the death-rate among the old was very high: above sixty they died like flies. The most neglected group are youths between fourteen and eighteen: they shoot up like young trees and need extra nourishment. The German

---

* Der Funkturm is the broadcasting tower for Berlin. The Russians have retained possession of it, although it is in the British sector.

† One of Wolf's friends is a doctor on the staff of a large Berlin hospital. She reports that half the cases show the symptoms of under-nourishment.

doctors are not so skilful in treating diseases arising from malnutrition and faulty sanitation, *e.g.* dysentery, as British doctors: they have not had Britain's colonial experience.

Whilst I am in the building I meet an officer whom I used to know as a youth in political life in London before the war. I try to adjust myself to realising that he is a major. He gives me a good introduction to the Socialist–Communist situation which I shall be investigating to-night. Taking Berlin as a whole, he judges the Communist Party to be stronger than the Social Democratic Party, and it has the advantages of an abler leadership and a Russian-provided press. The Social Democrats have no paper at all.* On the other hand, there is no doubt that the overwhelming majority of the Social Democrats are opposed to fusion with the Communist Party.

After dinner at the *Hotel Am Zoo* I talk for a time in the lounge with some of my fellow-pressmen. I begin to recover respect for my profession. Among them is John Anderson, of the *Manchester Guardian*, sensitive, serious, made uneasy by what he is seeing and hearing here. He never looks at home in this excessive comfort of our life, revolted by its contrast with the hunger around and concerned because the British are developing in Germany the rôle of the Raj in India—a race of conquerors in social standards and spiritual attitude. There is Solon, of the *News Chronicle*, a democrat and humanist to his finger-tips. There are American and Scandinavian journalists who have a broad, humanitarian view of things and don't give the Hamburg impression of just having a good time. I haven't the same feeling about the officers billeted here. Most of them are young and are gay and appear carefree. To-night they are eager to make the most of the beautiful summer evening, for tennis and boating. Night clubs will follow. I haven't it in my heart to blame them; they have known nothing since they left their schools except drab years of war. But one wonders whether it is really necessary to have so many of them, a bubbling white froth on the surface of the wretched life which is Berlin. Its people must bitterly resent the contrast of their laughing good health, their good living, their round of sports and amusements, with their own hungry misery, their cellar homes, their colourless existence.

FOUR SOCIALISTS FROM RUSSIAN SECTOR

The car takes me to a little house in the suburbs of Berlin. There I meet four Socialists from the Russian sector. They are

* The British have since issued a licence for the *Social Democrat.*

70

typical working folk: the kind of men you would meet in any Labour club at home. My talk with them is the most depressing experience I have had so far in Germany. All four have had long years in concentration camps under Hitler: one of them was arrested as early as 1933. They came through that experience with their spirits still aflame—but now three of the four are broken men. They had been able to stand up to the pressure of Nazism, but when on top of this, at the moment of their hope for liberty, came the pressure of the Russians, they could stand up no longer. Their spirits are crushed.

I shall try whilst I am in Berlin to get the full story of the Russian and Communist tactic to fuse the Social Democratic and Communist Parties. These four Social Democrats have no doubt about its purpose: it is to counterbalance the unpopularity of the Communists, due to reaction against the Russian Occupation and the unforgotten happenings of its earlier days, by the mass support which Social Democrats have. With the Parties fused, the Communists are confident that, with the help of the Russians, they can control policy.

I ask what are these methods of "pressure" which the Russians have exerted. It is painful to hear the answers, which are shot at me like machine-gun fire by the four men grouped about me. Russian military officers, I am told, attend all meetings of the branches of the Social Democratic Party. If any voice is raised against fusion—*Einheit* is the German word—the offender is summoned to an interview with Russian officials. If after this interview he maintains his opposition, he finds that his job has gone or he is evicted from his house. If he persists in opposition, he is deported to some distant part of Germany or even interned in one of the concentration camps where the Nazis also interned Socialists. Some technical charge of a formal character is made the excuse.

These are the general charges. I now get the personal stories of these four men separately. The first was chairman of his Social Democratic branch. He opposed *Einheit* despite the presence of two Russian military officers. He was then arrested and "softened" by interrogation. He agreed to resign his position as chairman and, under Russian orders, a supporter of fusion was substituted. He still quietly carried on his activity, however, and the Russians found his influence remained. He was again summoned for interrogation and accused of holding an illegal meeting of ten persons. He was threatened that all the ten who attended would be arrested unless he declared publicly for *Einheit*. Under the nervous strain of this pressure

71

and to save his comrades he agreed. He admitted to me that he had now lost all moral influence among his fellow workers. (I feel that this violence against the spirit of his personality is a worse crime than any physical torture could be.)

The second comrade has been allowed to remain in the Russian sector on condition that he gives up his political work, but in fact he is the only one of the four who is carrying on. He and a group of comrades cross into a Western sector night after night, holding their branch meetings there and maintaining contact with the free Social Democrats in other parts of Berlin. He cites an instance of deportation from his branch whilst it still met in the Russian sector. One of its members was a recognised economic expert. He has been exiled to Saxony.

The third comrade was also chairman of his Social Democratic branch. When it became obvious that opinion at the members' meeting was against *Einheit*, the Russian officer forbade the resolution to be put to the vote. Nevertheless, this comrade was appointed delegate to the conference of the Social Democratic Party in the Russian zone which was to decide the issue; thereupon the Russians prohibited him going and demanded that he should retire from all political activity. He continued as a Trade Union secretary, but only three days ago the Russians had declared that he was intolerable in this position and had nominated two candidates, supporters of *Einheit*, from whom the Trade Union should select a successor.

As he speaks, it is obvious that this man is still feeling the strain. For four weeks he has been interrogated by the Russians almost daily, and only the night before he was warned that he had better leave the district. "And I had two and a half years in prison under Hitler", he remarks. "Hitler still lives", one of the others comments. "No, Hitler is dead, but his spirit lives", he replies.

The last of the four has been district leader of the Social Democrats. He was deposed by the Russians and a new leader imposed. His influence continued, however, and one night he was arrested, taken by car to the Russian headquarters, and instructed to 'phone to the pro-Social Democratic paper in the British Sector, that his district was in favour of *Einheit*. He refused, and was released only on condition that he kept quiet politically. So far he has obeyed, but he speaks with vigour and I have the impression that his spirit will reassert itself.

I spend most of the time getting the stories of these men, but I ask about conditions in the Russian zone and sector. They describe the ruthlessness of the dismantlement of factories, railways, even houses. Contrary to my expectations, they say that the dismantlement is still going on. Factories are still being stripped, trucks and barges go loaded with articles and do not return. Cattle are driven from Mecklenburg and are fed on the growing crops *en route*. Potatoes are seized to make alcoholic drinks for the Russians. I must check up on this, because those journalists with whom I talked to-night are going to the Leipzig Fair which the Russians are staging next week to exhibit the industrial reorganisation in their zone. The stories of these men and the claims for the Leipzig Fair don't make sense.

I am sad as I return by car to the *Hotel Am Zoo*. I think of our enthusiasm for the Russian revolution, of the monthly supplements I had published in the *New Leader* describing the construction of its socialist society, its industrial and agricultural advance, its conquest of illiteracy, the new healthy life of its younger generation, the hope of this Socialist Sixth of the World. That there has been a great material revolution one cannot doubt; it is a tragedy that it should be deformed by this spiritual persecution which in essence, if not in degree, is the same as the oppression of opinion by Nazism.

WHAT GERMAN HOUSEWIVES COOK

It is late, but Wolf and I still have a session exchanging our experiences of the day. Wolf is seeing the life of the German people more intimately than I am. He is going to the homes of those whom he knew in the pre-Hitler days and is learning their story intimately. The discovery which excites him most is that the resistance movement to Nazism and the war was carried on much longer and more thoroughly than we had thought; we had been led to believe in England that it disappeared about 1942, but he has been talking to those who were engaged in it right to the end of the war. Wolf has gathered a lot of material about this historical chapter in Socialism's story, and I hope it will be published when we get back to England.

The part of Wolf's recital which moves me most is the description he gives of what the hunger means in personal terms. I've been hearing about calories and proteins: Wolf has seen what they mean in German homes and kitchens. He has been into one home to-day where there were actually potatoes (not officially distributed for some weeks); the family had bartered their cigarette allocation for them—one meal of potatoes for a months' cigarettes. The potatoes were fried with coffee grouts, kept from the previous day's *Ersatzkaffee*: the woman says that the grouts give the potatoes a "particular taste". This main potato dish was preceded by "soup". Wolf was present when it was made, and it consisted entirely of breadcrumbs and salt dissolved in hot water. The family had "tea" with the meal, tea made from pine tree needles. The recipe was published in a Food Facts column in the newspapers:

"You need 1 oz. of pine tree needles and 2 pints of boiling water. Appearance: very light, slightly green. Taste: slightly bitter. Preparation: The needles are washed, cut to tiny pieces and then boiling water is poured over them. After 3 to 5 minutes pour out the tea—not later, or the tea will become too bitter. Dry the needles and keep them airtight and in a warm place. In this way you can get a drinkable tea. Note: Experiments without cutting the needles to tiny pieces prove that you do not get the taste at all."

The *hausfrau* tells Wolf that other popular meals, publicised in the papers, are a vegetable dish made from stinging nettles and a salad made from dandelions. Potato peelings are collected, not for pig food, but for human food. A meal of potato peelings fried with onions (if they can be got somehow) is regarded as a great delicacy. The *hausfrau* stresses a point which I have not emphasised enough. The German rations (unlike ours) are the *total* food provision: except in the black market, no eatable whatsoever—except salt and vinegar—can be bought off the ration. Not only is all food in restaurants on the ration, but there is no food in the shops which is additional to the ration. When German people hear how much we can buy in the shops extra to our rations, when they hear what we can eat in canteens and restaurants without surrendering coupons, they say we aren't rationed at all: our food is just "controlled".

"They Died like Flies"

Wolf relates a tragic story, illustrating what I heard at Mil. Gov. to-day that the old people have died like flies. He came to Berlin with the intention of arranging for three old acquaintances to cross the Channel under the new Home Office scheme which allows close relations to join their folk in Britain. Of the three, he has found to-day that two have died in recent weeks. The first was a strongly-built man whose normal weight was twelve stone: he weighed seven stone when he died. The second, a woman, died from weakness due to malnutrition. Neither was sixty-five. Wolf has seen the last of the three to-night. She lives in the Russian zone, but crossed into Berlin with her daughter to meet him. Since he came to Germany nothing has stirred Wolf so much as this meeting. The old lady was half-starved in a concentration camp during the last

74

two years of the war, and she has been half-starved in "liberation" for a year. She was painfully thin and feeble, and the nervous reaction to seeing Wolf, and to the hope of joining her son in London, was so great that she had almost collapsed.*

Another significant thing: when Wolf went to visit one old friend to-day he found that early in the afternoon he and his family were all in bed. Were they ill? Oh no, they were weak with hunger and were conserving their strength. They told them that this is a general custom when the meagre rations have all been eaten.

We are tempted to go on exchanging experiences and opinions, but we have an early engagement to-morrow morning. We say goodnight. It is 2 a.m.

* See page 88.

THE SEVENTH DAY

May 4th, 1946.

OUR ENGAGEMENT this morning is with Dr. Wegscheider, the first woman to get her doctorate degree at Berlin University, friend of Keir Hardie, the Socialist head of education in Berlin and Brandenburg before Hitler. (You remember I left Wolf to find her yesterday morning.) The car takes us to the door of tenements flush with the pavement in a street not far from Lancaster House. The walls are badly knocked about. There isn't any glass in the window-spaces, which are still blocked with wood.

On the pavement children are playing, mounted on sticks between their legs for horses, their heads decorated with paper hats. The rhyme "Ride a cock-horse to Banbury Cross" comes into my head. Wolf talks to the children and lifts a paper hat from one of the heads. It is made out of a Nazi poster urging women to have more children! What does this mean? Are their parents Nazis or have the children got the paper from a dump? We don't pursue the point. The children are smiling at us, but they would be scared if, in our uniforms, we began to question them.

A WONDERFUL OLD WOMAN

Inside the passage is so dark that we have to light a match to find Dr. Wegscheider's flat, even though Wolf was here yesterday. She has no sooner opened the door than she is hugging me. When I can look at her I see a face that is lined, but which has great strength and a quality which I can only describe as calmness of spirit. Her hair is drawn back tightly; she is dressed drably, but with slim neatness. She guides us to her sitting-room with firm steps and her voice is full and clear. She is seventy-five, but has the personality of a woman of forty.

Her room is crowded with furniture and well-filled bookshelves. There are good pictures on the walls, classical and modern. There is a child's school desk. There are vases of flowers: lilac blossom. I examine the books on the shelves. They are mostly historical, philosophical, scientific. "Ah, the Nazis destroyed some of my most precious volumes," she exclaims. "My socialist library, in which there were many English works." I notice two magnificent busts in ebony on top of the bookshelves. The first is of Voltaire, given to her by a Jew before he killed himself during the Nazi persecution. The second is of the Greek god Bacchus, left to her by a Jewish woman who also committed suicide. "She wasn't a victim of the Nazi persecution," she explains. "She was rich and did not believe she was loved for herself, but for her millions. She was so unhappy that she took her life." We have been in Dr. Wegscheider's flat for three minutes, and yet we are talking as though we have known each other for years.

"I am so happy to be speaking English," she says radiantly. "I haven't spoken it for twenty years." I am taken aback. Her vocabulary is perfect: even the pronunciation (a more difficult matter) is good. She brings out photographs of her visits to England in 1908, when she spoke at a Ruskin College Summer School at Bournemouth, and in 1911, when she took her two boys to the Socialist Holiday Camp at Caister and attended a Suffragette meeting at Lowestoft. This last is a rich memory to her, because Keir Hardie took her to the meeting. She draws my special attention to the photograph of a group at Caister. She picks out Fletcher Dodd, the organiser of the camp, and Dick Wallhead, the pioneer Socialist propagandist, and his daughter Muriel. She knows that Dick was returned to Parliament and hears excitedly that Muriel is now M.P. "How wonderful!" she says, her face lit with delight. "The whole world did not retrogress with Hitler. In England you went forward."

I ask her how she lives. "As I've always lived," she replies. "I teach. The children begin to come at half-past seven, and all day I have one or two of them in here, teaching them." That explains the school-desk. "And you can get along?" I ask. "Of course! I am as strong as a young horse. When I awake I could pull oaks out of the ground! I do everything—clean my rooms, do all my own washing. Get along? Yes, gloriously. I have no money, but I do not like money. One-third of my lessons I give without payment, because the parents of the children need it more than I do. I'm told I ought to charge the others five or six marks, but why should I?—I am old and I haven't any teeth. I charge them two or three. They tell me I'm stupid, but it's people without money I like." "And your rations?" "Why, I get *extra* rations for teaching! I don't feel hungry."

This woman astonishes me more and more. She reminds me

77

of someone at home, and then she uses a phrase which completes the identity. "I am the granny of the German Socialist Movement," she says—the same phrase that one has heard from Mrs. Bruce Glasier many times. The likeness grows as Dr. Wegscheider continues to talk. She tells us that she has added religion to her Socialism—economics are not enough, ethics without God are not enough. She recites a terrible story of the first hours of the Russian Occupation. She was held outside the door whilst a girl taking refuge in her rooms was raped ten times. Twice the girl fainted, but the soldiers went on. Yet she hastens to speak well of the Russians. The first Russian she met was kind and good—and he was shot in her own room. The battle was going to and fro; the Russian burst in, then the Germans who shot him, then more Russians. She characterises the different troops in a few vivid words. "The Russians—lots of them are lovable boys, tender, helpful, kind: but they like shooting." "The Americans—they, too, are just boys, overflowing with life, gay, showing off, but so human." "You English? —so polite and reserved and self-disciplined, the most civilised of all."

Communist Slogans on Walls

It's been an inspiration to meet this brave old stalwart. As we go out to the streets again, Wolf tells me of the Karl Marx school which used to be under her jurisdiction, and how markedly she influenced all the scholars, particularly those who grew up to be Socialists in their 'teens. Wolf wants to visit some friends who live about a mile away: we decide to walk. The bomb-damage here is about the same as in London, but Wolf tells me that in large parts of the Russian sector which he visited yesterday it was as complete as, and even more extensive than, the destruction in the working-class areas of Hamburg. We approach a street which is "closed". The underground which had run beneath it is fully exposed by a breach 100 feet in length. We stop and read the posters on walls and the fronts of damaged shops. There is an extraordinary show of Communist posters—a hundred to one of any other Party. Their appeal for *Einheit* is reminiscent of the nationalist and totalitarian appeals of Hitler. I note down their most frequent slogan: "*Ein Ziel, Ein Weg, Einheit*". (One Goal, one Way, one Party.) Under one of these posters has been chalked the old Nazi slogan: "*Ein Volk, Ein Fuhrer, Ein Reich*." (One People, One Leader, One State.) The imitation was irresistible!

At the home of Wolf's friends—they are Jews who have been

taken out of a concentration camp and put into a flat previously occupied by a Nazi family—we meet a young sergeant in the British Military Police and accept an invitation to have lunch at his mess. It is a roomy flat, rather bare, reasonably comfortable, but without any beauty. Half-a-dozen sergeants billet here, with German girls to do the housework, cooking and waiting. We have a good meal with plentiful helpings. We have a look at the sergeants' bedroom—a large room with four beds. I begin to classify bedroom billeting. Officers—one bed to the room: Sergeants—four beds to a room: Privates—eight beds to a room.

THE INSIDE STORY OF "EINHEIT"

Wolf goes off to seek out more old-time comrades. For the first time I make visits which I cannot record. I spend the afternoon getting the inside story of *Einheit* and, at the request of those who gave it me, I must not reveal their identity. I go back to the *Hotel Am Zoo* and prepare a report on the whole subject. What I write is based on authoritative documents and personal statements of whose truth I have no doubt. It is a long and deplorable story, but it must be told. It has not been published by anyone else. Here is the report:

In the first days of the Russian Occupation of Berlin a year ago, the relations between the Social Democrats and the Russians were good. Indeed, when it was known that the other Powers were to take over sections of Berlin, the Russians proposed to the Social Democratic Executive that they should transfer their headquarters to the Russian sector in order to obtain their political protection. They did so.

Nevertheless, from the first the Russians weighted their support heavily to the Communists. The Social Democrats asked for paper to publish a journal. They were told that it was doubtful whether any papers would be allowed. The next morning the Communist Party paper appeared! It was a month before the Social Democrats had a paper, and then it had to compete with eight papers which followed the Communist Party line. The Russians gave the Communists sufficient newsprint to reach a circulation of four millions. The Social Democrats were allowed only one-fourth of this, and the same proportions were allotted to posters and literature.

The Russians began by appointing Communists to the leading administrative positions throughout their zone and sector, but they had in many cases to substitute Social Democrats because the former proved unequal to their duties. Despite the privileges which the Communists enjoyed, everyone acknowledged that the Social Democrats were much the larger Party. Indeed, right into the autumn there was no doubt that the Social Democrats had mass support in Berlin, whilst the Communists were regarded as the puppets of the Russians, who at that time were still unpopular because of the happenings which had occurred when their troops entered the city.

What exactly is the policy of "Einheit" and what is behind it? This is its background and development as revealed in the documents and evidence I have secured.

When, after twelve years of suppression the German workers were at last allowed to form political parties again, there was an instinctive desire for working-class unity. Both Social Democrats and Communists recognised that their failure to act unitedly in 1930 and 1931 had opened the door to Hitler. The obstacle to unity was their different conception of Socialism, but when on June 12, 1945, two days after *Marshal Zhukov* allowed political parties to be formed in Berlin, the Central Committee of the Communist Party declared against the forcible imposition of the Russian system in Germany, and called for the establishment of a Democratic Republic, the Social Democrats felt that this obstacle had been removed—and themselves proposed unity. On June 19 the Communist Party also declared for unity, but when the representatives of the two Parties met, *Wilhelm Pieck* and his two colleagues who had come to Berlin from Moscow declared that fusion was premature. The Parties therefore organised separately, whilst acting together on many issues.

In the autumn the Russians had a shock. The elections in Austria and Hungary went overwhelmingly against the Communists. From this moment they decided to destroy the power of other Parties, so that when the time came for elections in Germany the disastrous defeat of the Communists in Central Europe should not be repeated.

They turned first to the bourgeois Parties, insisting upon the resignation of the leaders of the Christian Democratic Union and the Liberal Democratic Party. Then they summoned the Social Democratic Party Central Committee to meet the Communist Party representatives. Prior to the meeting the Social Democratic Executive and the district leaders from the Russian zone and Berlin discussed the position, and decided that they would oppose the fusion of the two Parties in one zone alone. They laid it down that amalgamation should take place only if it applied to the whole of Germany and was the democratic decision of a conference of mandated delegates from branches in all the zones.

When the Social Democratic Central Committee met the Communist Party representatives, they found they were in the presence of two representatives of the Russian Military Government and an official stenographer.

This made it difficult for them to speak out openly, but *Gustav Klingelhöfer* had the courage to protest against Russian intimidation, quoting the case of a Social Democrat in Saxony who, because he was opposed to fusion with the Communists, had been kidnapped, shot in the neck and left for dead. The final outcome of the meeting was that fusion was not endorsed except for a platitudinous declaration in principle for an ultimate united workers' Party, but it was agreed to prepare a common electoral programme.

The Social Democrats thought they had won their point, but in fact they were out-manoeuvred. They had acknowledged publicly their desire for the ultimate union of the two Parties. The inevitable result was that the Communists asked, "if eventually, why not now?", and the Russians began to apply pressure still more openly. Social Democratic branches in the Provinces were only allowed to hold meetings jointly with the Communist Party. The Russians insisted upon profusionists occupying all the leading administrative positions in the Social Democratic Party in their zone. In Thuringia *Dr. Brill* was compelled to resign his chairmanship of the Party, and his place was taken by a Russian nominee, Hoffmann. When on January 6, at Rostock-in-Mecklenburg, a crowded Social Democratic meeting passed a resolution in favour of an all-Germany referendum on the issue of fusion, the Russians instructed the editor of their newspaper not to publish a report and forced him to publish an article by a Communist which referred to all those who opposed fusion as "reactionaries" and " saboteurs". During the same month two leading members of the Social Democratic Central Committee, Grothewohl and Dahrendorf, were refused permission to visit the British zone. The Committee had taken up its head-quarters in the Russian sector to obtain "protection". Now they found themselves prisoners.

On January 15 the Social Democratic Executive issued an instruction that no local amalgamations of their branches with the Communist Party should take place and that fusion could be decided only by an all-Germany congress. *The Russians prohibited the publication of this instruction and forbade speakers to refer to it; in some cases speakers who contravened were arrested.* By the end of January any Social Democratic officials who opposed fusion felt the hand of the Russians. Some were removed from office, some were arrested, some were forcibly removed to other districts, some were actually interned in the Oranienburg and Sachsenhausen camps, where anti-Nazis have been interned under Hitler.

A TRAGIC LETTER

I have got so far drafting the report when Wolf returns from his visits and enters my room. I put a question to him which nonplusses him for a moment: "Which would you say, Wolf, is the most tragic document you've had in your hands in Germany?" He considers for a moment and then answers: "That letter from the prisoner in the War Criminals' Trial written on the eve of his sentence." "Yes, that was tragic, but I think this is more so." I pass over to him a letter which I have been reading.

It is a letter from the secretary of the Magdeburg section of the Social Democratic Party to the Central Committee of the Party (Magdeburg is in the Russian zone. The Party had 52,000 members). The letter describes the success gained in the

Trade Union elections: the Party won a considerable majority of the offices—996 Social Democrats against 667 Communists. Whereupon the Russian military authorities ordered that the election results should be ignored and the offices shared equally with the Communist Party. The Social Democrats had to give way.

Similar pressure was exerted throughout the district to compel the acceptance of Communist policy. When local Social Democratic officials demurred, they were summoned to interviews with the Russian officials, who interrogated them for hours and sometimes for days. If opposition was maintained, threats replaced argument; if it was still maintained, arrests confirmed the threats.

Party officials were shadowed everywhere; their speeches were reported to *General Kotikov* in Halle. If they opposed the Communist line, they were prohibited from speaking.

Up to this point the Magdeburg letter contains little new. It only records local instances of the general policy of Communist intimidation which I heard from those four Socialists in the Russian sector last night. But now comes the conclusion of the letter—and here is its pathos.

The Magdeburg Social Democrats report to the Party Central Committee in Berlin that they can no longer stand out and that they will have to merge with the Communist Party, and they advise the Central Committee to face the force of circumstances and expedite fusion with the Russian zone.

Wolf reads the letter and says: "Yes, it is the same tragedy as in the letter of the Nazi war criminal—compulsion to do something which you do not believe". He leaves to write the notes of his visits. I continue my report:

HOW "EINHEIT" WAS IMPOSED

The Magdeburg Trade Union elections were typical of what happened throughout the Russian zone and sector. In a dozen of the leading towns of Saxony, 174 Social Democrats were returned against 17 Communists. The first Works Council elections in Berlin gave 79 Social Democrats and 18 Communists. In 44 Berlin workplaces, 127 Social Democrats and 56 Communists were elected to the Factory Committees. When the Russian military authorities saw how the elections were going against the Communists, they issued instructions that the appointment of Trade Union officials should not be governed by vote.

The Social Democratic Central Committee in Berlin now had to decide the issue put to them by the Magdeburg comrades—should they stand out for their democratic principles and for Democratic Socialism or should they knuckle down to Authoritarian Communism?

Weak leaders like *Max Fechner* gave way—Fechner, the only surviving member of the pre-Hitler Central Committee, "a glad-hander only wishing to be on good terms with everyone". *Dahren-dorf* stood out; this was noteworthy because he had always championed Russia's policy in the Eastern zone, saying that it was the only part of Germany in which Socialism was being applied by means of land distribution, the socialisation of industry, and the power given to the Trade Unions. *Grotewohl*, the chairman of the Central Committee, able, a good reconciler, a fine speaker, wobbled. In December he announced that he would dissolve the Party rather than see it lose its independence; he often repeated that only an all-Germany conference could decide the issue of fusion with the Communists. But in January and February great pressure was placed on him by the Russians. *Colonel Tulpyanow*, of the Russian Information Services Control, *Ambassador Simenow*, and *Marshal Zhukov* saw him in turn, telling him he must choose between East and West. *Zhukov* demanded a decision by the end of February, hinting that if the decision were favourable, Russia would increase food supplies and aid the economic revival of Eastern Germany.

Grotewohl decided to make a tour of the Russian zone. When he returned, he told how the Social Democratic organisations were crumbling beneath the Russian pressure and how men who a fortnight earlier had been assuring him of their loyalty to an independent party were now begging him to hasten fusion so that they could be left in peace. Concluding that fusion was inevitable, he decided to push it through as speedily as possible.*

On February 11, he declared for unity with the Communist Party and for a conference, *covering the Russian zone and Berlin only*, to bring it about.

On the day Grotewohl *announced the intention of the Social Democratic Central Committee to amalgamate, six new cars were delivered by the Russian military authorities to the Party Headquarters and twenty food parcels were received from* Marshal Zhukov *for distribution among "needy members of the Party".*

It soon became evident, however, that the rank and file in Berlin would not submit to fusion with the Communists without a struggle. On February 17, three crowded meetings of Social Democratic members passed votes of "no confidence" in the Central Committee. On March 9, at a conference of Berlin Social Democratic officials, *Grotewohl* was howled down and some 1,850 voted against fusion and only 150 in favour. During March, in seven different Boroughs of Berlin, 1,039 delegates voted against and only 174 for fusion; at meetings in Spandau, Wilmersdorf, and Pankow (Russian sector), 96, 83, 93 per cent respectively, voted against fusion.

Grotewohl and the Central Committee then attempted to crush

* There are some who think that Grotewohl is still a sincere Social Democrat and that he will yet prove this.

opposition by expulsions from the Party. On March 12, *Germer* and *Neubecker* were expelled; on March 19, *Swolinsky*, *Kiaulen* and *Schulz* were expelled; March 22, *Aussner*, *Lohrenz*, *Arndt* and *Ganschow*. The District Committees of Charlottenburg and Schoeneberg were declared dissolved after anti-fusion votes had been passed.

The Berlin Social Democrats then decided to hold a referendum on the issue of fusion. *Grotewohl* and the Central Committee were alarmed. They applied to *General Bokov*, of the Russian Military Government, for 40 tons of paper and 400 gallons of petrol—and got it. They used the Russian-controlled press of Berlin to vilify the opponents of fusion as reactionaries and supporters of foreign trusts. Thousands of posters appeared on the walls and millions of leaflets were distributed.

The opponents of fusion got no paper from the Russians, of course, but on the basis of democracy secured limited supplies from the Military Governments of the three other sectors in Berlin. *Grotewohl* and the Central Committee issued instructions to Party members to boycott the referendum. On March 31 it took place. In the Russian sector no polling booths were permitted to open; in the non-Russian sectors, out of 33,000 members, 23,500 voted. There was no doubt about the result. The figures were: Against Fusion, 19,529; For Fusion, 2,937. That is, nearly 7 to 1 declared themselves in favour of the maintenance of a Party which stood for Democratic Socialism. At the same time, the great majority were in favour of united action with the Communists on agreed issues. A second vote taken on this subject yielded a majority almost as large.

Fusion is now proceeding in the Russian zone and sector, though there is evidence of many Social Democrats standing out courageously against it. The Communists are pursuing their usual tactics: they have issued instructions to their Party members to continue as a group within the United Party and to act together on all occasions for the Party line.

In the non-Russian sectors of Berlin the Social Democrats have reorganised and elected a new Provisional Committee. The leadership is at present with new men—*Franz Neumann*, a young proletarian, *Germer*, a young intellectual, and *Swolinsky*. These are the three men, particularly Neumann and Germer, who have been courageous enough to stand out from the first. But many of the older leadership, including *Paul Loebe*, a former Minister, *Dr. Otto Suhr*, until recently head of the Central Administration for Trade and Supply in the Russian zone, *Dr. Ostowski*, a former Mayor of Berlin, *Gustav Klingelhoefer*, an accomplished economist, and *Frau Annedore Leber*, whose husband was killed after the July 20 plot, are also coming out on the side of the independent Party.*

In the non-Russian zone one can scarcely find a Social Democrat who is in favour of fusion with the Communists. Their aim is

* I met Annedore Leber, charming and able. Whilst her husband was in the concentration camp, she became a dressmaker under an assumed name and was so successful that all the high ladies of the Nazis became her customers. She had a savage delight in overcharging them.

Democratic Socialism and, if they had not been convinced before, the methods of the Russians and the Communists in attempting to impose fusion would have convinced them that Free Socialism and Authoritarian Communism are fundamentally different things.*

German Girls Gate-Crash the Sergeants' Club

When I finish writing this long report, I take a quiet stroll to enjoy the cool evening. By chance I meet the young sergeant who was my host at mid-day. He insists on being my host again and takes me into the Sergeants' Club, a few doors away. It is a most attractive place. The restaurant is on the ground floor: glittering chandeliers, tables for two and four with pink cloths and wine glasses. (Sherry or port is 6d. a glass.) Above is a lounge with magazines, papers and books, and a billiard-room. The sergeant tells me an amusing story of two girls who came in one evening dressed in uniform. It was a strange uniform, but no one can keep up with all the uniforms, and they were served their meals. When, however, on reaching the coffee stage, they ordered the meal all over again, the waiter thought it time to investigate. It was found that the girls were Germans, serving in some Welfare Service near Hanover. They had "jumped" the train to Berlin and "braved out" the best meal they had tasted in their lives!

Civil Service Clerks are Explosive

It is time for my "date" with the explosive civil service girl at her NAAFI—the girl who is going to give me the "low-down" on the conditions of the staff. The car takes me to the "compound": an estate of large grey buildings isolated by cross-bars spanning the road and sentries in their little boxes. The reason for this isolation I don't know. It can't be the girls, because their NAAFI is shared by soldiers.

The NAAFI is a drab barn of a place, with a bar at one end. My girl is sitting at a long table reading a newspaper, and when I join her other girls gather round, and soon they are pouring out their grievances. A sergeant, a red-faced Scot carrying a pint of beer, asks whether he can listen in. He does, with a good deal of scepticism. One of the group is the secretary of the Staff Welfare Committee, a dark, clean-featured, clear-minded young woman. She puts the case, with frequent help from Miss Explosive and the others—and Miss Explosive has periodically

* I hope some day I shall be able to acknowledge the source of the greater part of this report.

to be hushed into quietness by her amused colleagues. All of them are members of the Civil Service Clerical Association, and we have hardly got going when Hill, a member of the Executive, coated and carrying a bag, appears on the edge of the group. He is just leaving for a meeting with staff representatives in the British zone, and he asks the girls and me not to implicate the Union by what they say. Very good, the Union is not implicated.

The main complaint of these civil servants is that when they volunteered to come they expected to be treated as civilians, and they are being increasingly treated as "other ranks" in the army. They illustrate their case first by accommodation. When they arrived ten months ago at Frankfort in the American zone they had separate bedrooms and two or three of them shared a sitting-room. In Berlin they started with nice flats. Now they are to be transferred to a badly-blitzed warehouse, with four, three and two to a room: a barracks. The warehouse will accommodate 800, including troops: only sixteen will have single rooms. Originally it was intended to house 1,600 in this warehouse; it was only as a result of protests by the Welfare Committee (a rank and file committee from the messes) that the number was halved. They were told on joining that after a year conditions would improve, but in fact they are getting worse. Is this to go on for the fifteen years of the Occupation?

They complain of the conditions of their travel when they go on leave. The trains are cold, dirty, with wooden seats and often with no lights. Frequently they have to stand long distances. Some of the girls describe how they have gone from breakfast at 9 a.m. to tea at 5 p.m. with nothing to eat. I think of the luxury of the officers' travel, the sleeper I enjoyed from Hanover to Berlin, and my conscience is pricked. They complain of the medical facilities. They are under the military medical service, have to go on the military parades when they report sick; there is no special diet in the Sick Bay. Their committee offered to pay for Benger's and similar invalid foods, but it cannot get permission.

The Welfare Committee secretary is anxious to be reasonable. She lists the advantages over home conditions: free entertainments, free travel, free post. But she insists that these do not compensate for the grievances they have been voicing. The fundamental point is that they are losing their civilian status. No one has put it better than Miss Explosive when she accosted me at Lancaster House: the claim is being made that the

British administration is being civilianised, when in fact the civilians are being militarised.

I am sympathetic. But the problem is not simple. The real complaint of the girls is an indictment of the conditions of the Other Ranks. The right thing to do is to insist that these conditions shall be ended for all. I have no doubt that the grievances about travel and medical treatment can be put right, but when one comes to accommodation my mind goes to those German families who have been turned out of their homes to cellars and shelters in order to provide accommodation for British personnel. This is one of the difficulties of any Occupation, particularly when so many houses have been destroyed. My impression is that if the stupid policy of a long Occupation is maintained, its clerical staff will have to be largely recruited from Germans. In the Mil. Gov. offices already a large German staff of typists and secretaries is employed.

I put these views to the girls, and they are in the mood to argue them all night, but it is late and the car is waiting. "Shall I give you my opinion of what these lasses have been saying?" asks the Scottish sergeant. He curves his hand round his mouth and puts it close to my ear. "It's all ——" he whispers. Well, it's not that, but the civil servants will do well to unite the soldiers' grievances with their own.

Back At My Hotel

It is late when I get back to the hotel, but I look in at the bar before going to bed. A genial giant gets into conversation: he had been in the R.A.F. and still wears its uniform, though he is now attached to Transport. To-morrow morning he is starting out with six Russian journalists on a tour of the British zone, and he offers to give me a lift to Düsseldorf—our next destination—but that's impossible because of engagements. It would certainly have been interesting to travel with the Russian party.

The waiter in the bar is an attractive young Negro. Remembering that Hitler classed Negroes even below Jews, I ask him how he fared during the war. "Not so badly," he said. "You see, my mother is German." I find, however, that he was restricted to half rations.

I go up to my room. The clock downstairs pointed to one, but I stretch out on the settee for a last smoke. The 'phone rings. When I lift the receiver I hear Wolf's voice at the other end. "May I come to see you?" "Of course." Wolf is distressed when he enters. Yesterday I noted how he told me of three old folk whom he planned to get to England.* Two had died. He had begun to arrange for the departure of the third. To-day he has heard that she died last night a few hours after he met her.

* See page 75.

THE EIGHTH DAY

May 5th, 1946.

TO-DAY WOLF and I are meeting Franz Neumann and Karl Germer, the young leaders of the Berlin Social Democrats who have had the principle and courage to stand out against *Einheit*. We are to meet at Germer's flat in central Berlin, and the problem is how to get Neumann there. He is the Mayor of Tegel, a distant suburb in the French sector, and there is no transport this Sunday morning. I can use a Mil. Gov. car, but there is a rule that civilians must not be carried. I put the difficulty to a man of experience. He advises risking it. The object of the rule is to discourage officers from taking girls for joy-rides. If I am stopped by military police I can explain that I am transporting the civilian for press purposes, which is true. So I risk it.

The streets are different this Sunday morning. There is a stream of people outside the *Hotel Am Zoo* going to the cinema next door. Whenever we pass houses with a garden attached, we see the family engaged in raking the earth and, if they are lucky enough to get them, sowing vegetable seeds. (I am told that it is easy to get certificates for seed-purchases, but very difficult to find the seeds to purchase.) As we get farther out, I notice how often men are engaged in hacking out roots of trees for fuel—whether the trees have been destroyed by gun-fire or cut down during the winter I don't know. The men dig deep trenches round them to get the whole roots. The most noticeable feature in the streets is the number of people who are cycling out with sacks folded over their back wheels. They are food-scrounging, the driver tells me.

There is no evident difference in the French sector except the uniforms of the soldiers and the frequency of the *tri-color* flag on official buildings. We reach the suburb, turn down a narrow lane lined with pleasant bungalows, and pull up at a cottage-house standing in its own little garden. Neumann, his young wife and child might be any British working-class family: this home could be found in Britain a hundred thousand times. I am welcomed like a brother.

Neumann's name occurred in my report yesterday on *Einheit*: he was one of the first to stand up to the Communists and to the Social Democratic leaders when they went over to the Communists. Riding in the car to Germer's flat I get him to tell me his personal story. We pass a large prison building. "I was in there two years under Hitler—and two weeks under the French." "Under the French?" I exclaim. "Yes, but that came later. Let's begin at the beginning. Where *shall* I begin?" I suggest from the occupation of Berlin by the Allies.

"I met the first Russian jeep," he says. "Amidst the falling buildings and whilst the shooting was going on, I stepped into the street to shake hands. The behaviour of the first Russian troops was good—the others, about whom you've no doubt heard, came later. I at once began to build up the Social Democratic Party illegally. The English followed the Russians in my district, and then the French. I had already been appointed Mayor before the French came and was presiding over a Council one afternoon when it was reported that soldiers were beating up the people in the streets. I couldn't believe it, but went out to see, and there, sure enough, a bloody battle was going on. I shouted that I was the *Burgomeister* and appealed to the French soldiers to stop, but I was attacked myself. On the ground beside me was a girl with a bleeding head. I picked her up and took her to the First Aid Post. When I came back I nearly fell over a man who had lost a leg in the war and who had been bludgeoned to the ground. I was helping him to the First Aid Post when soldiers flung themselves on me, beat me up, and broke my arm. They arrested me, made me stand facing a wall for ninety minutes and stole everything in my pockets. This was on October 15, 1945, five months after the end of the war."

"Whatever was the explanation?" I ask. "I don't know to this day," replies Neumann. "The story goes that whilst some French soldiers were playing football, two revolvers and a wallet were stolen. This apparently led the soldiers to make the assault. It was the private action of the gendarmerie; the higher authorities knew nothing about it and they sent an official apology to our Council meeting next morning. That was at 9 a.m.—one hour later I was arrested, questioned about the stolen revolvers and wallet, and taken to prison. And not only prison—the second day I found myself in a dark special cell without food!" "Why?" Neumann laughs. "I was given the job of scratching the dirty whitewash off my cell wall with a spoon," he says. "They complained I had not done it cleanly enough, and accordingly sentenced me to two days in the punishment cell without food."

We arrive at Germer's flat. He is a young man with a round face and domed forehead: a schoolmaster or civil servant or journalist, I should say, though I omit to ask. His young wife brings us some ersatz coffee to drink and leaves the four of us—Wolf is here—to talk in a large living-room. I am eager to hear the end of Neumann's prison adventure. "You tell how I got out," he says to Germer.

"A fortnight after Franz was taken to prison," he begins, "a delegation of French Socialists arrived, including the wife of Daniel Mayer, the Party secretary, and the Editor of *Le Populaire*. 'Who organised your illegal work under Hitler?' they asked. 'Neumann,' was the reply. 'Who re-formed the Party after Hitler's fall?' 'Neumann.' 'Who is your Mayor?' 'Neumann.' 'Where is this Neumann?' 'In prison.' It was the delegation from Paris who liberated Franz."

We settle down to a political discussion. Apparently there are still some restrictions on free speech. Twice a week it is Neumann's duty as *Burgomeister* to visit the French Commandant. He has been given the instruction that there must be no reference in speeches to the frontier question, neither on the East nor on the West. In particular, there must be no reference to the Ruhr or the Rhine. A similar instruction was given about the posters for May Day: they must not contain slogans about the frontiers. The English, I am told, took the same line as the French on this.

The *Einheit* issue has created difficulties between the Russian and Western Allies. Britain and America, probably for reasons of Power Politics but avowedly on grounds of democracy, have opposed the Russian imposition of fusion on the Social Democrats. They permitted the Social Democratic referendum in their sectors and provided a limited quantity of paper to meet the Russian avalanche of Communist posters and leaflets. At first the Four Powers (including the French) agreed that there should be no posters for the proposed fusion Party—the S.E.D.—as it had not been recognised, but nevertheless the Russians allowed them in their sector and three weeks later authorised them for the May Day demonstration, which they converted into an *Einheit* demonstration. Germer gives us more particulars of the Russian pressure for *Einheit*. Grotewohl, who was the Social Democratic leader, was publicly promised that if the German workers supported fusion 3,600 of the 4,000 factories which were to be handed over to Russia under the Potsdam Agreement would be returned to Germany. In a letter Grotewohl was also assured that a Workers' Government would be established in Eastern Germany and that work and wages would be plentiful, because the 3,600 factories would be given orders for a Five-Year Plan of Russian rearmament. Despite this, Germer confirms the reports I had from the four comrades from the Russian sector that industrial dismantlement is proceeding. Indeed, he says that its systematic organisation is just beginning. The early dismantlement was so clumsy that most of the material was spoiled or destroyed. Now the job is being done more carefully. He asserts that even factories which Germans have rebuilt since the war are being dismantled and that at all stations on the Berlin circle railway in the Russian sector there are large loads of articles for despatch to Russia. He instances a sugar refinery and a printing works which have been dismantled during the last fortnight, and describes how German workers have been refused rations until they have dug up cables to be sent to Russia.

This leads Neumann to make two remarks. The first is that the *Burgomeisters* in the Russian sectors have absolute power over food distribution and they use it nakedly for political purposes. Unless a worker joins the Communist Party there is little chance that he will be classed as a "heavy worker" and get the extra rations. Special gifts of food are made to encourage workers to turn out at political demonstrations. Those who marched behind the *Einheit* banners in the May Day demonstration, for instance, were given soup, bread and sausage rolls—an irresistible bribe. The second remark arises from Germer's description of the industrial situation in the Russian zone. He points out that things are reaching a crisis in the other zones and sectors. In the French sector of Berlin, for example, factories will have to close down within eight weeks unless raw materials come in. Neumann thinks that the British and Americans are managing better, but I remember my interviews at Mil. Gov. headquarters yesterday morning, when I was given a similar warning about the low stocks of raw materials.

Cigarettes Solve Domestic Crisis

It is time for lunch, but we have not finished our talk. A domestic crisis arises. Where is Neumann to get some food? In great distress, Mrs. Germer says she hasn't enough food to supply a meal and we are not allowed to take a German civilian to the *Hotel Am Zoo*. If Neumann is to get a meal in a café he must surrender coupons, and he hasn't any. The solution is found in cigarettes. Mrs. Germer gives the necessary coupons to Neumann, and I give her Players, for which she will be able to get a good deal more than the coupons would have allowed her. This is the nearest I have yet got to a black-market transaction!

At the *Hotel Am Zoo* I have a coffee with John Anderson, of the *Manchester Guardian*. He tells me that he is going to the Leipzig Fair, where the Russians are staging an exhibition of the industrial recovery in their zone. Industrial recovery? What, then, is the truth about the dismantlement of which I have heard this morning? I am the more puzzled because I hear that the Russians have got a typewriter factory going just outside Berlin and are producing machines at 350 marks each, against the 3,000 marks which they cost on the black market. The truth apparently is that the Russians are following a double policy. They are dismantling factories whose equipment they want in Russia: they are restoring factories whose goods they need in Russia.

How Will the Germans Vote?

Wolf and I return to Germer's flat. Everyone at least has had some food. We turn to political prospects. Germer urges that the division of Berlin into sectors should be ended. Instead, the whole city should be treated as a fifth zone, under an Inter-Allied Commission. Then he is confident the Social Democrats would have a good chance in the forthcoming elections. "When will the elections be held?" I ask. They cannot tell us. The British want them as soon as possible, the Americans in September, the Russians in December. Pieck, the Communist leader, is against early elections. He says the process of German "re-education" must go on for a time. Our comrades laugh as they report this. They have no doubt that Pieck means that the people must be "re-educated" from their "anti-Russianism" and the Communist Party given restored popularity by its camouflaged union with the Social Democrats in the new (and old) S.E.D. I report that a well-known British journalist has expressed the opinion that 70 per cent of the German people would vote Nazi in a free election. Neumann and Germer ridicule this. "The German's don't want another dictatorship," says Germer, "either Nazi or Communist." But he warns us that there is a growing tendency towards political neutrality, indifference and scepticism, and that this will grow if under the Western democracy hunger persists and un-employment increases because of industrial chaos: immediate chaos through absence of raw materials and longer term chaos through the dismantlement proposed by the Potsdam Agreement.

Our talk turns to the inner condition of the Social Democratic Party in Berlin. Neumann uses a striking phrase: "Our present Executive is a Kindergarten." The older leaders, even when sympathetic, are at present standing aside: the leadership is young and new. The average age of the Executive is well under forty, and a census of the membership in the non-Russian sectors shows that the average age is forty-four—a remarkable fact after thirteen years of Nazi régime and complete suppression of the Party. As we end this talk, I am full of admiration of the courage of these young leaders. Their deficiencies, which I would describe as the absence of a thought-out positive policy and an over-reliance upon the Western Allies, arise from their long isolation from responsible political planning and their need for some external support as an off-set to the Russian support for the Communists; but both constructive thinking and self-reliance will come if opportunity for their development is given. It is a great thing that belief and action for democratic Socialism live so strongly in Berlin, and these two men, Franz Neumann and Karl Germer, together with Kurt Schmidt, whom I did not meet, should be honoured by us because it was they, above all others, who were brave enough to stand out against Russian pressure when the older leaders, some by surrender, some by silence, failed.

In the Russian Sector

It is late in the afternoon. Wolf goes off to search out more old-time comrades. I take Neumann home by car. Our driver takes us through part of the Russian sector: a little foolhardy this, because Neumann has no right to be in the car and if we were pulled up by Russian military police they would certainly regard him as a capture.

We drive to *Unter den Linden* through the *Tiergarten*. This beautiful park, with its avenues of trees lined with statues, has become a wilderness. It was the scene of the fiercest Russian attack on the centre of the city, and not one in a hundred trees stands. Pathetically a few of the old statues stand: there is some old Emperor on his horse, but the rump of the horse is a gaping void. We see the Reichstag on our left and Hitler's Chancellery on our right, their condition of destruction familiar from photographs. We pass through Brandenburg Gate into *Unter den Linden*—the last time I was here was in August, 1931: that shattered building was the café where I read of Mac-Donald's desertion from the Labour Party and his premiership of a National Government. We turn left and thus out into the French sector. The propaganda for *Einheit* in the Russian sector is remarkable: not only posters but great red and white streamers hang across the road. The last of these is five yards from the "frontier" line of the French sector. One cannot enter or leave the Russian "territory" without being urged to back the new Party.

The trek of cyclists on the roads is now in the opposite direction. Most of the back wheels carry laden sacks. Another thing catches my eye—no eye could miss it. Everywhere there are lilacs—great bunches of them tied to the bike handle-bars and bunches almost as large carried by every other person one sees walking along the pavements. Never in England have I seen such a profusion of flowers.

The Nazi Who Left His Diary

I return to the hotel. Over dinner Wolf gives me an exciting account of a visit to a Communist friend from which he has just returned. The house had previously been occupied by a Nazi, among whose papers Wolf's friend had found a diary which outdid in its record of brutalities anything read at Nuremberg. The diary has been handed over to the Berlin police (Com-munist-controlled) and is no doubt now in Russian hands, but many papers, not yet examined, remain. What is more, Wolf has got the present address of the Nazi, in a small Westphalian town. "I'm looking him up," says Wolf, "and I'll return to Berlin when you leave for England and follow the thing through."

At the end of our meal I ask one of the P.R. Officers what is the tipping system at the hotel. "Tipping?" he exclaims. "Tip Germans! A year ago we were trying to kill them. You don't think we now tip those we failed to get?" I decide to double the tips which I had previously in mind.

We catch the train for Bad Oeynhausen before ten o'clock. As I tuck the sheets round me in the sleeper, my conscience is again sensitive about the lower grade civil servants and the "other ranks" sitting or standing in the crowded third class.

THE NINTH DAY

May 6th, 1946.

WE ARE met at Bad Oeynhausen by the same *Volkswagon* and driver who brought us here from Hamburg. Car and driver have now been placed indefinitely at our service. We drive to Herford, a pleasant little rural town, which is the Head-quarters of P.R. in Germany, and have breakfast at Warcor-mess, which I suspect was a small hotel before, and perhaps during, the war. Whilst we are eating, a young English officer accompanied by five Russians enter—the correspondents, I guess, with whom I had been invited to travel. After the men had seated themselves, a drab little woman comes in. She goes all round the table, shaking the men by hand in turn, just like a child saying good morning to a Victorian family. The Russian journalists are an interesting group, an older man with close-cropped hair, a picturesque young man with a bush of black fuzzy hair and flashing eyes: very handsome. The woman is the interpreter. The English officer is perfect Public School—courteous, platitudinous, facetious. What a colleague for the Russians!

ON THE ROAD TO THE RUHR

We start on our drive to Düsseldorf, centre of the Ruhr. Just before we turn on to the autobahn we meet a gang of forty men marching under the guard of armed police. Our driver tell us they are prisoners, not prisoners of war but men sentenced for offences in Germany, some by the Nazis, some under the British administration. They are employed on road-making, heavy demolition work, and similar jobs—I wonder if they see much difference between Nazi and democratic régimes. The autobahn carries us quickly into the beautiful countryside of Westphalia. It is the most prosperous-looking agricultural country I have seen. The hills roll away like the Cotswolds, deep green with growing corn and yellow with mustard plant. Dotted among the wide fields are red-bricked farmsteads, necklaced with trees. Everything is trim and in good repair. One has no sense of the poverty which so often mars rural areas.*

* The headquarters of the various departments of Mil. Gov. are in little

Our driver begins to unbend to our friendliness. He tells us that during the war he drove Nazi officers and since the war British officers, but he has never before met officers who treat him as a human equal—and carry their own bags! He is slight and small—bright-eyed and quick like a brown mouse, and always ready to find fun in any situation. I guess his age accurately: thirty-four. He was in the transport service on the Russian front and describes how, during the retreat, any soldier found five miles from the line was immediately shot or hanged: he saw them shot by the roadside or hanged to trees. We explore his political background. He acknowledges that he voted Nazi in 1933. He was twenty-one and his father was out of work. The Social Democrats had failed and he had no confidence in the Communists. What was there for him to do but vote Hitler? he asks. For a long time he kept his faith in Hitler: his father got work, he got work, everything seemed better—he didn't realise that this was just "war preparation" prosperity. He had become disillusioned during the war, but so far he hasn't got any new political convictions to replace the old. (Wolf and I will have to see what we can do about this!) We wonder about the liberty which is allowed him as a prisoner of war: he could escape any time he wanted. He says some drivers have escaped into the Russian zone—and taken their *Volkswagon* with them!—but he calculates that he's as well off now as he could be in any job: he has no family and likes running about the country, and his ration is one-third above the minimum.

We drive perhaps for three hours and then the *Volkswagon* glides down a descending arm, makes a horse-shoe bend, under-crosses the autobahn, and joins a second-class road which has the advantage of bringing us nearer to the homes and lives of the people—cottages, inns, churches, even a one-track railway, with a little puffing engine which tugs a string of open-sided cars. We continually pass lorries—not only army lorries, but German. The former are not allowed to carry civilians: the latter are packed with civilians and their belongings, bundles of clothes, pots and pans, sometimes bits of furniture. They make a depressing picture. The driver tells us that most Germans are travelling like this because of the difficulty of getting on trains. Lorry owners advertise that they have trucks going to this place or that; or people queue at the lorry starting places.

Westphalian towns and a large proportion of British troops are stationed here. This explains why many soldiers write home saying the Germans have enough food.

We enter the Ruhr valley. It is the first time I have been outside its towns, and the scene is not what I expected. I had thought of the Ruhr as unrelieved blackness, but here is a lazy river running through meadows, with only occasional chimneys and grubby mills and mines. I am reminded of the valleys of Yorkshire and Lancashire between the moors. Hagen is the first town we enter : it is heavily blitzed and the rubble has been hardly touched. Then Wuppertal, a long, straggling town with massive destruction, which might have been committed the night before. Wuppertal is famous for its suspended railway— an ungainly contraption which runs for a time above the river, dirty by now, and then over the main street, the cars hanging from a rod. And so we reach Düsseldorf, a large city with busy streets and big buildings, many in ruins.

Mil. Gov. H.Q. is the biggest building of all—previously the H.Q. of the Ruhr steel industry. Outside are British Tommies on sentry duty, marching a few steps to left and right, turning, clicking heels, carrying guns. This is the first time I have seen this play-acting, since I have been in Germany. Inside, there is a huge board with notices of offices and officers : I want to see Tom Agar, English Trade Unionist and Socialist, who is the Industrial Relations man for the North Rhine region. We find that he is in another building. Before leaving we admire two huge mural paintings, illustrating the steel and mining industries of the Ruhr. Ive not seen anything better since in America.

The car takes us to Agar's office, but he will be out for an hour. I notice the same building houses the Jewish Relief Organisation and its secretary, Mary Wise. She is the daughter of Frank Wise, a distinguished Parliamentary colleague of mine in 1929, whose early death was a great loss to the Socialist movement. She immediately invites Wolf and me to dinner at the Yacht Club and says she'll arrange for us to visit the Social Democratic Mayor of Düsseldorf afterwards. This sounds good. Meanwhile we have to fix our billets. After some crisscrossing between departments, we are directed to the Officers' Transit Mess at Garath. It's twelve miles away, so, our beds fixed by 'phone, we put off going until after the evening's engagements.

FIRST CONFERENCE OF THE METAL WORKERS

We return to Tom Agar's office and find him in. He has soon bustled us into the car again. When we called earlier he had been at the first conference of the Metal Workers' Union and he is eager for us to see it. We climb the stairs of a large building, and on the top floor find a hall with four hundred delegates sitting like a phalanx: the massed delegates, few over middle-age, sitting square in their black suits, give an impression of strength and solidarity. I am asked to speak, and, contrary to my expectation, they prove to have the same emotionalism as the inhabitants of the coal and steel valleys of South Wales. When I refer to comrades who shared the platform with me in Germany fifteen years ago and who have been done to death by Hitler they angrily shout "Pfui", and as I conclude a man in front jumps up singing *"Wann Wir Schreiten Seit' an Seit'"*—and in a twinkling they are all on their feet singing. One thing is evident: they have a high regard for Agar, and Agar is proud of their Trade Union emergence. This is good to see: a sense of working class solidarity which transcends not only racial difference, but the difference between the Occupying Power and the Occupied people.

I have decided to cut out my talks with Mil. Gov. "highups" at Düsseldorf, not because the interviews at Hamburg and Berlin have not given valuable information, but because time here is short and I particularly want to go to the mines and contact the miners. One very unofficial interview I squeeze in, however, with a Mil. Gov. official whom I knew as a Socialist before the war and who has fought in Africa and Italy and is now a major. We go to a Church Army canteen for a chat. I find his experience in army and occupation has moved him far to the Left.

We are brought tea by a German girl. She tells us she has come from Breslau, and her eyes light when I say I have been there and that its Socialist leader, Eckstein (he was dead in a concentration camp within a few weeks of the Reichstag fire), was a friend of mine. She recalls her parents speaking of him. We ask where her parents are—she has no idea: they succeeded in getting her away from Breslau when it was annexed by the Poles, but themselves remained to save their home. Her letters to them are now unanswered. I take down particulars and promise to have enquiries made.* The girl is so friendly that I ask her wage: a thing I am always reluctant to do. She replies 55 pfennig an hour, that is a little under 3*d*. The wages are paid by the Düsseldorf City Council, not by the British authorities.

* The Friends' Committee for Refugees and Aliens is trying to trace the parents.

Over cups of tea my old-time comrade tells me exactly what I want to know before visiting the mines—the story of the North German Coal Control which bosses them. He is devastatingly critical. The headquarters are at Krupp's villa at Essen, and it's evidently his view that the Krupps spirit still haunts the Villa. He emphasises that the Control, which is an inter-Allied authority representing the British, French, Belgian and Dutch, has absolute responsibility for getting and distributing the coal: Mil. Gov. has no voice at all. The actual management in the mines is unchanged from Nazi days.

That's the set-up: my friend proceeds to describe the policy. The Control demanded about 80,000 miners. Its requirements satisfied, the food rations were cut! Immediately production fell, because the miners took days off to go to Minden to buy potatoes for their families (who were excluded from the higher ration). Faced by reduced output, the Control demanded the conscription of all physically-fit men between eighteen and thirty-five years, except skilled workers in occupations sponsored by Mil. Gov. The demand was conceded and a German Commission was formed composed of representatives of the supplying and receiving ends, mining people, and doctors from insurance societies. Its job was to tour the Labour Exchanges of the neighbouring areas and call up all available men. Everything was done in hush-hush secrecy, but when the Commission reached Wilhelmshaven there was nearly a riot. The town had been employed on work for the British navy; when the shipbuilding yard was destroyed there were mass unemployment and widespread discontent. An opportunity for the Commission! It ordered a quota of 500 men for the mines from Wilhelmshaven, but when the Labour Exchange Manager instructed the selected men to go they objected so violently that he had to call in police protection.

Despite the secrecy, the news of the Wilhelmshaven riot spread like wildfire, and in all the neighbouring districts the men between eighteen and thirty-five began to disappear. Of the men called up, half didn't turn up. Then it was decided that the men should be kept under guard after medical examination until transferred to the mines: the result, 50 per cent stayed away from the examinations. The men who disappeared became refugees, without food tickets, scrounging what they could from the land. The men who were held were put in trains and locked in until they got to the mining towns, where they were "decanted" to huts which, it was alleged, had not been cleaned since they housed Russian prisoners in Nazi days. Everything was indescribably filthy; the blankets verminous, the food uneatable. Permission for their families to make visits was refused. Again 50 per cent of the men deserted.

I listen with incredulity to this story. Not a word have we heard of it in Britain, despite the visit of Trade Union delegations to the Ruhr. As my friend goes on with his story, it is evident that the Coal Control could have provided plenty of material for a report by these delegations. It is aggressively anti-Trade Union. One of its high spokesmen has declared openly that the Control must discourage Trade Unionism because of the repercussion on British miners: if our pit-workers came to feel sympathy towards the Ruhr miners as fellow Trade Unionists difficulties might arise. I am told how a British officer of the Coal Control had visited the Industrial Relations section of British Mil. Gov. and issued the ultimatum that the Control would not tolerate interference from Trade Unions: the functions of the Works Councils would be limited to welfare matters. (Exactly the same as in Nazi days!) One of the Control's District administrators issued instructions for the appointment of Works Councils which completely ignored the Mil. Gov. direction that they must consist of elected representatives, and in the same District (it is No. 7) an order was given that no Trade Union notices must be posted on the mine premises: strong disciplinary action was threatened if the order were disobeyed. When the Regional Controller of the Ministry of Labour for Westphalia—a German—went to investigate welfare conditions at a mine, he was run off the premises!

An Evening with the Socialist Mayor

It is time to go to dinner at the Yacht Club. We pick up Mary Wise and Tom Agar at their office and drive along the bank of the Rhine, a broad but dreary river here. Its bridges were destroyed by the retreating Germans and have been replaced by temporary crossings over linked barges. In the water, boats lie on their sides sunk by gunfire as the Allied forces nearly caught the enemy. The Yacht Club is posh and the food, as always in Officers' Clubs, better than at home. A lively orchestra is playing and a few couples dance. Our meal over, the four of us drive to the Mayor's flat, and for once my rôle is reversed. The large-built Mayor and the friends whom he has invited insist on plying me with questions rather than answering mine. It is a revelation to find how even important officials are starved of information as to what is happening in the outside world.

THE MANSION OF A NAZI COAL-BARON

Nevertheless, there is one interesting bit of information which I pick up. There have been several Trade Union delegations to the Ruhr. Walter Citrine and Ebby Edwards accompanied the first, and both made a good impression. Citrine refused to allow Mil. Gov. officers to be present when he interviewed the German Trade Union leaders: he would not say a word until they had left the room. This caused a great sensation. As for Ebby, I am told the Ruhr miners loved him. He made them feel that he was one of themselves. Of another Trade Union delegation I did not hear the same praise. Its leader, I am told, treated the German workers' representatives as though they were criminals browbeating them, permitting them to put only one question each and answering curtly. At the end of the interview, one of the German Trade Union leaders, who had never bowed his head to the Nazis and who had been for years in a concentration camp, said he had never met anyone more like a Prussian officer. I felt ashamed as I heard this story.

It is late when we leave for our mess at Garath. Our driver is upset because he had not been able to get food coupons as in other towns. "I shall have to find a girl-friend in the Food Department," he remarks, with his flashing smile. "Don't bother", we retort. "We'll order you a lunch". We escape from the ugly destruction of Düsseldorf, skirt a lake in front of a spreading Schloss (as a boy I built toy palaces like this with red and white ornamental bricks, probably "made in Germany"), and enter a tree-lined drive which circles before the door of a mansion. We wake up a sergeant and he guides us up marble stairs to a vast bedroom furnished like the country houses of the British aristocracy. We ask the sergeant what we have hit. "A Nazi coal-baron accommodated his mother here," he tells us.

THE TENTH DAY

May 7th, 1946.

THE NAZI coal-baron must have held his mother in high respect. A more beautiful place I have rarely seen. French windows lead from our bedroom to a terrace which overlooks a wooded garden almost too lovely to be real. There is a background of chestnuts, rhododendrons, copper beeches, weeping willows, elms, all in their richest spring colours. Beneath them flows a stream which falls splashing over rocks to the left and broadens to a lake to the right. Paths wind through the trees and cross the stream by little white wooden bridges. The birds are whistling like an orchestra, and among their notes I recognise the call of the nightingale, though it had not wakened me in the night.

Breakfast is served by German girls in a wide-windowed room at small tables with white cloths and dainty cups and plates. At another table are three officers; two men and a woman. Breakfast consists of peaches, two fresh eggs, toast and a portion of country butter the size of a golf ball. On a plate is a day's ration of eight cigarettes—worth 40*s.* in the black market—for each of us. At our request we are supplied with a generous luncheon packet: we shall not need it, but it will compensate Rolf for his missing coupons. After breakfast I wander about the garden, whilst Wolf explores among the staff. The car arrives, but neither of us wants to leave this paradise for Düsseldorf.

TRADES UNIONISM IN THE RUHR

In the car Wolf reports the results of his exploration. There is a staff of twenty to run this mansion—a sergeant and eight privates, three German men and eight German girls. No wonder we were well-tended: there were "four servants" for each guest! Among some of the German staff he found more open Nazi sympathies than he had before come across. A girl said that, whatever one thought of Goering, he had shown political courage at the Nuremberg trial.

We drive to Agar's office and I obtain the facts about Trade Unionism in the Ruhr. They are better even than at Hamburg.

The number of members has reached the huge total of 301,366, and it pleases me to hear that all the 14 Unions are organised on an *industrial* (rather than craft or general) basis. The first instinct of the workers here was to set up One Big Union to cover all industries and trades, but after discussion they rather reluctantly came down on the side of Industrial Unionism, accepting it as the best alternative instrument—first to fight for immediate demands and, second, to prepare for ultimate workers' control. I am excited to hear this. It reveals a *socialist* consciousness which promises well.*

Agar is anxious for us to meet the Trade Union and Socialist leaders here, particularly Hans Boeckler, of Cologne, whom he describes as the Tom Mann of the Ruhr. Boeckler is seventy-three,† but he has tremendous virility of body and mind and is as militant a Socialist as he was at twenty. During all the Hitler days he carried on, hiding in cellars until he was caught and taken to a concentration camp. Agar does some telephoning, but cannot fix any appointment until the afternoon, and by then we shall be away on our visit to the mines. He arranges for us, however, to see Adolfi, the Social Democratic manager of the Labour Exchange, a new and interesting field of investigation, and he deputes his English-speaking German assistant, an earnest young Socialist named Paefgen, to go with us on the day's tour. Tom Agar's office is all-Socialist. His Mil. Gov. colleague is a Fabian, who, like every Labour Party member I've met in Germany, has advanced far to the Left whilst he has been here.

* British Trade Unionists will be interested in the details which I got. They may be compared with the Hamburg particulars given earlier. Here are the Unions, their memberships, and (in brackets) the number of meetings held during April:

Metal	74,165 (53)	Food and Drink	11,212 (27)
Mine	64,651 (27)	Building	6,644 (88)
Transport	21,652 (27)	Printing	3,003 (9)
Public Employees	20,546 (63)	Bank and Insurance	2,314 (19)
Chemical, Paper and		Wood and Timber	1,463 (3)
Pottery	20,356 (14)	Commercial	1,117 (50)
Textile, Clothing and		Agricultural	220 (3)
Leather	16,326 (75)	Clerical—still in Phase I	(6)

† I am given the ages of the Trade Union Officials. It is high, because men of experience have mostly been selected, and that means pre-Hitler Trade Unionsts. The average age is 52·5 years, and 38 per cent are between 50 and 60. The group between 40 and 50 includes 30 per cent. The 60 to 70 group contributes 19 per cent and 3 per cent are actually over 70. On the younger side, 9 per cent are between 30 and 40 and less than 1 per cent under 30. I hear that Tom Agar is taking classes to train younger Trade Unionists.

The Labour Exchange is a large, well-appointed building, standing behind a courtyard fronted by a prison-high wall. A large tree in the court removes the prison-like effect. I am a little surprised to find that the manager's office is also his bedroom: an indication of Düsseldorf's overcrowding. He is sitting at a table, with his young girl-secretary at his side and a Mil. Gov. officer opposite. The Mil. Gov. man is one of a team of eight inspectors who go the rounds of the Labour Exchanges. He offers to withdraw whilst we have our interview, but Adolfi says he has nothing to hide and the officer stays. Adolfi is seventy-two but he is strong and straight in body, speaks with lively vigour and certainly does not hide anything. He is an experienced administrator. For many years before Hitler he was a City Councillor in Düsseldorf, graduating to the Social Democrats through the Communist Party. For six years he was in Russia.

The allocation of labour through the Exchanges is restricted severely by the demands of Mil. Gov., which must be met before workers are permitted to go to other industries. Priority is given first to the British administrative staff and then to firms working for Mil. Gov. There is no chance to direct labour into other essential channels or to plan economy. The Mil. Gov. demands are made through a department known as the Civilian Labour Unit, which insists on skilled labour to a greater degree than can be supplied and issues sudden orders—"withdraw 100 men from this factory"—which dislocate production seriously. Unemployment, as elsewhere, is low and is mainly among men who are not fit for mining, demolition and building.

As we leave the Labour Exchange we are held up by an excited, gesticulating group of people who surround the tree in the courtyard. They are shouting angrily, pointing to a large notice which is pinned to the trunk of the tree. Wolf and I stand on tiptoe at the back of the crowd and strain to read the notice. Here is an exact translation:

"*Former officers of the Cavalry are requested to report to Room* 313 *in order to be attached to a British Unit.* 3.5.46."

The people see our uniforms and turn on us. "They were the worst Nazis," shouts a worker at me. "They were Junkers," shrieks a woman. I've not yet met such passion in Germany. The Exchange Manager comes out. The crowd accosts him angrily. "I am not responsible," he insists. "It has been put up by orders of the Military Government."

I go to the nearest 'phone box and ring up the Civilian Labour Unit of Mil. Gov. One of its high-ups explains that it is intended to use the German Cavalry officers as grooms and stable-boys. "O.K.", I reply, "but why put up a poster which gives such a wrong impression to the German people?" "We are not concerned with the impression made on the German people," he retorts. "It is our job to get the officers." At that I go over the deep, forgetting that I am in uniform, and that I'm talking to a senior officer. "This is the daftest thing I've met in Germany so far," I exclaim. "Are you running your department as Nazis or democrats?"* I turn to Wolf. "I bet we haven't heard the last of this," I remark.

A German Socialist Sums Up

We are lucky enough to meet one of the leading Düsseldorf Social Democrats outside the Exchange. He had been at the Metal Workers' Conference yesterday, but I stupidly forget his name. We retreat to a little public garden and sit on a bench under trees and talk. The Social Democrat takes a serious view of the situation. "Hitlerism was born in an economic crisis when people were hungry," he begins. "It is the same to-day. Under Hitler we had bombs, but we had food. To-day the people are beginning to forget the bombs, but they can never forget their want of food. The death of democracy in Germany was due to the fact that our representatives went to the League of Nations and brought nothing back. Now we go to the Military Government and bring nothing back." He goes on to say that if the food problem can be solved there are grounds for hope. The greater part of the German people want to break completely with Nazism. They believed in it, but are now utterly disillusioned and want to turn to new ways. Of the alternatives offered to them, Democratic Socialism has the greatest opportunity. "They don't want Communism. They don't want Red Storm Troopers in place of Brown Storm Troopers. The Communist Party used to be strong in the Ruhr and would probably have captured it except for the Catholics; but now its influence has declined. If your Labour Government can give food to the people, you will see the triumph of Democratic Socialism here. Even the middle class is ready to come over."

* I hear afterwards that the outburst was reported to the Security Police and detailed enquiries made about me.

"And the youth?" I ask. "The younger generation who have only known Nazism?" "You've hit the real problem," he replies and re-emphasises the view which the socialist students put at Hamburg. "In my view we must treat them sympathetically. You will be wrong, and we shall be wrong, if we put them outside the pale because they have been Nazis. We must open the door to them and invite them to an understanding of Democracy and Socialism." We ask for his view of the British Military Government. He recognises the immediate need for the Occupation of Germany, but not for military government. "The military can order," he observes, "but they cannot govern."

Only Four Days' Supply of Flour

We drive to an Officers' Club for lunch, leaving Rolf with our luncheon packet and with time to make another effort to collect his coupons—"that or the girl-friend" he grins. We have a date at the Club with Mary Wise and a woman from Czechoslovakia who is in charge of "displaced persons". Whilst waiting for them in the lounge I get into conversation with a Mil. Gov. officer who is in charge of flour distribution in the Ruhr. He is living from hand to mouth—or perhaps it would be more accurate to say that the people of the Ruhr are. Three days ago he feared he might be without any flour whatsoever, but he has contrived to get some delivered from Antwerp by barges. Now he has four days' supply, and whether he will get more in time to provide bread next week he doesn't know. No wonder Mil. Gov. takes a serious view of the food situation! We take a respite from serious topics over lunch. Our minds are tired and our hostesses are engaging.

Rolf is despondent when he arrives back with the car. He hasn't got the coupons. We set out for Oberhausen and the mines. "Stop," I say before the car has gone a hundred yards. "We'll pay another visit to that Labour Exchange and see whether the riot has broken." But all is quiet on the Labour Exchange Front. The poster has gone from the tree and the crowd has dispersed. "We had orders to take it down ten minutes after you left," an official says.

Weakness of British Aid to Unions

In the car I think about Mil. Gov. organisation in relation to the Trades Unions. I didn't question it at Hamburg, and I didn't see it at Berlin, but here I begin to have doubts about it. Sherwood at Hamburg and Agar here are not Trade Union officers, but Industrial Relations Officers. Theoretically it is not the job of such officials to identify themselves with the Trades Unions, but to hold the balance even between employers and workers. It seems to operate all right when there's a Sherwood or an Agar, but, of the twenty Industrial Relations Officers in the British zone, *only six are Trade Unionists !* The rest are seconded military officers, many of whom have no knowledge of Trades Unions, or Ministry of Labour officials, many of whom have no sympathy with the organised working-class. At Bad Oeynhausen, the H.Q. of Industrial Relations, there is only one Trade Unionist—and he is a junior. At Berlin there is not a single Trade Unionist. At Münster, only one. Moreover, even when the Industrial Relations Officers are Trade Unionists, they are subordinate to the Civil Service heads, merely an incidental arm of the Man Power section. This doesn't seem to me to be good enough.

In the U.S. zone there is a Labour Adviser to every military commander. In each case he is a representative of the C.I.O. or the A.F.o.L., the two large American Trade Union organisations. When confirmed by the commanders, their word goes. They issue the directives and the Civil Service carries them out; but in the British zone it is the Civil Service which issues the directives and the Trade Unionists (when there are such) carry them out. In Agar's office I met a French Trade Union Officer, an enthusiastic Socialist. Apparently in the French zone there is, typically, no single method of organisation, but in this officer's district—the South Rhine—the responsibility rests with him. He is not subordinate, and his job is to encourage the development of Trades Unions.

My thought carries me on to a comparison of the British political set-up with the Trade Union set-up. Austen Albu is Political Adviser to the Commander-in-Chief. He is independent of the Civil Service; he can approach the Minister in Whitehall directly as well as the C.i.C.; when endorsed, his recommendations operate. The politicals are clearly getting a better deal than the Trade Unionists. I must take this up with John Hynd and the T.U.C. when I get home. Trade Unionists ought not to tolerate the present position.*

* I raised this whole question with Mr. Hynd on my return. He is himself a Trade Union M.P., and is naturally concerned to do all he can for German Trades Unionism. He tells me that Austen Albu has been appointed Deputy President of the "Government Sub-Commission", of which the Industrial Relations Division is a part. This is good news, but not, in my opinion, enough.

I look out of the window and see we are passing through Duisburg. "Stop!" I shout excitedly. One of my best friends of the pre-Hitler days is the secretary of the Social Democratic Party here: I must see him at all costs. Eberhard Bruenan was a member of the Socialist Workers' Party. In 1931, when I last saw him, he couldn't have been more than twenty, but he and his girl-friend were a joy to meet: utterly devoted to the socialist cause and fearless. They were both arrested in 1934; he was sentenced to fifteen years' hard labour and she to four years'. Neither of them was liberated until the defeat of Hitler —the girl had been taken straight from her prison to a concentration camp. Last summer, eleven years after their trial and separation, they married, and are now again working together for Socialism in this town of Duisburg.

We get out and enquire for the S.P.D. office. It's in a back street, one of a row of working-class houses. We mount rickety stairs to a front room on the first floor and find a typist at a table, a group of youths, and behind a desk sits Eberhard. We gaze at each other for a few seconds and then he leaps up and clasps me. For a time he can only laugh and wring my hands, whilst the others watch bewildered. Eberhard is no longer the care-free young crusader I knew fifteen years ago, but it is evident that his long years of imprisonment have not destroyed his spirit. He is distressed that I cannot stay to visit his home and his wife and that there is no time for a political discussion. In a few sentences he indicates his dissatisfaction with much of the personnel and policy of the S.P.D. and his desire to see more Leftward action. He introduces me to the youngsters in the room (late 'teens and early twenties) and tells me he is giving them lessons in Socialist history, theory and policy. The best kind of "re-education"! I hate leaving Eberhard Bruenan, but it is great to have seen him after all the years and to find him unbroken.

TALK WITH THE MINERS' OFFICIALS

Oberhausen must have been a dreary town at its best. Now, severely blitzed and uncleared, it is a desolate waste. The Trade Union headquarters are in a side street, three rooms with two kitchen tables, five chairs and a typewriter. The miners' officials are like many of ours: stocky, reserved, slow-speaking. For a talk we go to a pub. It's as drab as English pubs built fifty years ago, but that's the only similarity. No crowd jostling along the bar, no line of people propped on ledge-seats against the wall: here are tables with entire working-class families grouped about them. They have evidently come, like we have, to talk rather than to eat or drink; there is not a sign of anything to eat and the "beer" has next-to-no alcohol and tastes like medicine.

We surround a corner table, and the talk at least is plentiful and good. These miners' officials may be slow, but they know their stuff. When I ask them what they want done with the mines, their answer is immediate: Nationalise them under Trade Union control. I hear of a military commander who treats the German workers according to the worst traditions of colonial administration. He sits with feet on his desk and a riding whip at his side; he will not allow a German to sit in his presence.* Trade Union activity depends a great deal on these local commanders. Permission has to be obtained for meetings and it is the custom of some commanders to issue a permit only on the preceding day, so that it is impossible to do the necessary advertising for large meetings. A number of the commanders, I am told, placed every obstacle in the way of the May Day demonstrations.

A VISIT TO THE PITS

In two cars we drive to the Concordia pits, Nos. 2 and 3. We pass miners' houses: a row, one-storey high, like a broken black wall—I've seen the same thing in Scottish villages; better, four-storey tenements, badly bombed, the windows all out; detached huts, sometimes with holes in the roofs, sometimes in the walls. We get a rather chilly reception at the pit gate, but when the manager arrives he is friendly—the miners' officials say that is why they selected these pits: it is doubtful whether we should have got on to some other pit premises. The manager speaks with evident sincerity about the tough times the miners have had: the bombing during the war, their hunger now. Their special ration is a lot higher than others, but it is still below what their heavy work needs. The thing that gets them down, however, is the hunger in their homes. They have to eat their extra ration at the pit and are searched to see that they take nothing to their families. It is the manager's opinion that worry over their wives and children prevents the miners from getting value from their own canteen

* A Mil. Gov. officer confirmed this later.

meals. "Food doesn't keep up your strength if you are worrying," he says.

We start on our tour. Most of the surface buildings are in ruins: chimneys and the water-tower are completely down. The manager reports that the two pits had 104 direct hits and 15,000 incendiaries! I see a new use for slag-heaps. Deep shelters have been dug into their sides.

We go into the much-repaired boiler-sheds. There is no need for the manager to invite the men to gather round: they are curious and, when they learn that we are Socialists, they speak freely. I feel comradeship with them at once. Except for their tongue, they are just like our miners at home—the miners of South Wales, Yorkshire, Scotland, whom I know so well—not only just the same in appearance, with their blackened faces and coal-dusted clothes, but the same in spirit. As everywhere, they are the most militant among the workers. "We don't care who our bosses are, German or British," says a big fellow, with approval from the group about him. "Both exploit us in the same way—treat us as slaves, give us just enough food to make profits for them. I tell you straight, we'll fight British bosses just as we fought German bosses. The Nazis put me in prison, and I'm ready to go back there if necessary. We are against all bosses—we want to get rid of them altogether." I smile as his forthright phrases pour out. I might be in the Merthyr valley! A smaller man, with eager eyes, breaks in. "We've been promised for fifty years that we shall get the first place in industry because our job is the hardest. We're still at the ninth place! Do you know what our wage is? Two hundred marks a month —five pounds in your money. A pretty reward for our job! A Ruhr miner lives ten years less than any other workers. You'll hardly find one who isn't mutilated somewhere about his body."

There is no stopping these men. A third is streaming out bitter utterances. "Sunday work—a seven-day week—is compulsory for key workers," he says. "Do you know that until a few weeks ago we had no Sunday ration? Forced to work— and no food in your belly to work on! What we get now is only thin soup, and it is taken from the pit's normal supply which has not been increased. To get anything at all on Sunday, we have to eat less on Saturday." A fourth man is concerned about workers' rights and he confirms what I've already heard about the Works Councils. "The District Colonels are little Fuehrers," he exclaims. "Each of them makes his own decision, and they all decide differently. Right up to a fortnight ago, some of them refused to allow any Works Councils in their districts. Now they have to recognise them, under the new Law 22, but they put every kind of obstacle in the way. Are these Colonels the best present your Labour Government can make us?" They all laugh, and we laugh too. Others talk about their bombed homes, roofs still letting in the rain, walls with open cracks, furniture in bits. "And when we take time off to do repairs, we get punished as absentees." They all begin speaking together about their families, the hunger, the children shoeless; but I tell them we'll go and see for ourselves. They storm us with the addresses of their homes. Before going, we shake hands all round. They grip tightly. Agar told me that it actually takes a month to get German workers to see him, the Socialist, through his Mil. Gov. uniform. Well, we've broken through our uniforms in half-an-hour with these miners.

In the Homes of the Miners

I want to go down the mine and meet the men at the coalface. The manager is ready that we should, but warns us that they are working an hour's distance from the shaft. Alas, we can't spare that time. Instead, we are taken to the miners' tenement homes, probably the best of them. We go round to the back, mount to the first floor, and are in the kitchen-living room of a miner's family. Again, I might be in Yorkshire. This woman, drably and neatly dressed, homely, cheerful despite her unending struggle, might be any Yorkshire miner's wife. Her kitchen, for what it is, is shining, scrubbed and spotless. Her husband, only forty-three but looking much older, comes out of one of the two bedrooms. He has been twenty-seven years in the pits, but stopped work six weeks ago with silicosis. No pension has come through yet—they are living on savings; when the pension does come it will be 70 marks a month—35s. I don't know how many children there are: it's difficult not to fall over them, and the woman is obviously pregnant. She tells us that all the family never stop being hungry. The children are only getting meals twice a week at school, sometimes only once a week, and it consists of soup made from three biscuits and a small slab of chocolate. She can't get them shoes. I notice that one girl, about twelve, is wearing bits of wood, cut out to the shape of the foot, with straps across. Another girl is shoeless. She has one pair, but she saves them for Sundays.

We don't have to knock at the door of the second tenement. The family is grouped on the landing, listening, and they invite .

us in. The man is at the pit, but a son of twenty, who is on the night-shift, stands by the side of his grey-haired mother. She shows us his hand, with one finger a stump, for which he gets no compensation because he can still work. "I didn't want him to go into the mine," she says. "I wanted him to be a joiner or a builder. But it was the mine or the army, and I'd rather have him at home than in the army." How many times I have heard English mothers say that! Two younger children stand around looking at us with wide-opened eyes. "My grand-children," she says. "Their mother lives on the floor above." I ask whether they go to school yet. "They go on alternate days because they have only one pair of shoes between them," the woman says. From the children themselves I find that each attends school only one day a week. This confession rather disconcerts the old lady, but her son is frank about it. "We only send them for the meal, and its never more than twice a week," he says.

The German "Bevin Boys"

We drive on to the "Bevin-Boys" barracks. I am now to have an opportunity of meeting the men who were press-ganged into the mines by the methods which the Mil. Gov. officer described yesterday, and to see their conditions. Barracks is the right word. I don't get a clear mental picture of them outside, but I have an impression of dusty yards without a tree or bush and of prison-like buildings. We enter one. It had been bombed, and a temporary roof put on: otherwise it was just a skeleton of a building. Going through the door, we are in a large, bare open space, a few stiff-backed chairs against the walls, a table in the middle—that is all. This is the common-room for the boys. The rest of the building is partitioned off for sleeping accommodation: twelve berths, like our war-time tube shelter berths, and metal lockers. Not a chair. I go in search of the lavatory accommodation. I find a bare, stone-floored place with four circular troughs: there had been a fifth, but it was shattered in the bombing. The latrines and W.C.s are in a similar place on the other side of the building: the seats are of earthenware and in a row down the centre of the stone floor, without any privacy. I can well imagine that this was a barracks for prisoners of war. I have spent three years in seven prisons, and I have never seen anything so colourless and comfortless. The best that can be said is that it's clean.

When I return to my companions in one of the partitioned compartments they are surrounded by about twenty young

113

men. They are as angry as the crowd round the Labour Exchange tree; they are shouting and their faces are bitter. As soon as I enter, half-a-dozen of them accost me. I can almost feel the ferocity of their voices as though it were physical: for a few seconds I am a little frightened, the first time since I have been in Germany. Usually I can follow German, but with three and four speaking at once and in strained voices I can make little of what they are saying. I explain that I am a Socialist: that means nothing to them—I am in uniform and British, and I am responsible for what's happening to them. They curse Mil. Gov. roundly: I tell them I have nothing to do with it and refer to the Unions. They curse the Unions, which have ignored them: they curse everybody. I don't think I have ever met men who have such a sense that everyone is against them.

With the help of Paefgen, Agar's German assistant, who comes over to us, we quieten down and I begin to get their story. First, they are angry about the way they were seized and brought here. One of them took over a small shop at the end of the war. He had just got it going. He was summoned for medical examination—and he has never seen the shop since. He was treated as a prisoner, and that is what he has been ever since. My memory goes to the forced labour which the Nazis thrust on thousands of deported men from France, Belgium and Holland, but I cannot refer to it: that hideous wrong does not make this slavery right. They complain of want of food: it is not enough for their hard work and growing bodies. They complain of their living conditions—as well they might.

The German Trade Unionists who are with us, Agar's German assistant, are as shocked as we are: they had no idea that things were so bad. They promise to take them up; I promise to take them up as soon as I get back to London; but I have the feeling as we drive away that we have not restored much faith to these Ishmaels. I try to imagine how diseased their frustrated personalities will become if they are left long like this.*

We take back the miners' officials to their office. Their assistant has urgent news for them, told with great excitement. Authoritative information has come from Düsseldorf that the British are mobilising Nazi officers. What can it mean—war with Russia? They see Wolf and me exchange smiles and look

* Tom Agar 'phoned me next morning that he would visit the boys and act urgently. He had contacted the Miners' Union. When I got back to London, John Hynd promised immediate enquiry.

enquiringly at us. We tell them the story of the Labour Exchange tree.

A Personal Adventure

I start out on my only personal adventure during this visit to Germany. A supporter of the I.L.P. has been appointed controller of one of the leading industries in the Ruhr. At home he had been an outspoken critic of the war-time practices of the largest British firm in the same industry, a firm so powerful that it has a virtual monopoly. When he got to Germany he found that his chiefs were representatives of the same firm, and he didn't get on too well with them. To that was added a personal complication. He fell in love with a German girl to whom another Mil. Gov. official was also attracted, and there was conflict. I don't pretend to know all the ins and outs of the story, but it ended—or, at least, as I was to find, the first *instalment* ended—with both officials being sent back to England. Before I left London I promised to look up the German girl and convey to her my friend's intention to return and marry her at the first opportunity.

When I reached Düsseldorf, however, I found that I had left her address behind. She had been employed in the Economic Section as a secretary, so I 'phoned its office and the corporal who answered knew me at once: he had been chummy with my friend and, though he didn't know the girl's address, knew her house. He was stationed a few miles outside the town. If I would look him up, he would take me to the girl.

So now we are on the way to the corporal. We have a marvellous drive, along a narrow yellow lane which bends and lifts and falls between stretches of young corn. The ugliness of the Ruhr towns is forgotten. We mount a height, and around us are dipping valleys and rising hills, green and yellow, with occasional groups of red farmsteads and cottages and grey churches. Somehow we feel on top of the world. The blue sky seems very near, just on top of the little hill which our car is approaching. Passing through a village we see a soldier in a strange uniform. Our enquiry brings a startling answer. He's Hungarian, a General. A prisoner? Yes, but like his regiment, allowed so much freedom that the German people in the neighbourhood don't know whether these strange soldiers are prisoners or part of the Occupying Force! Apparently they are Hungarian soldiers who don't want to return to their country whilst the Russians are there.

The Mil. Gov. offices where the corporal works are closed.

We cruise round the town to find the N.C.O.s Mess. It's a pleasant little villa. My corporal is waiting, and instals me at his side in front of a jeep. At first I wonder if I shall be able to cling to the seat, but soon I'm enjoying the spurts and the swerves and the rushing wind. We cross the river at Düsseldorf by the long, low bridge over the boats and come to the much-bombed working-class district of Neuss. I am glad someone who knows the way is bringing me. I would never have found the girl's home through all this wilderness of rubble.

The houses here are of the cottage type, divided into an upper and lower flat. The corporal evidently knows the place well (has the girl a sister?), and mounts the stairs and knocks at the door with confidence. The girl opens it, shows me into a comfortably furnished little sitting-room and brings me tea. The corporal has slipped into the kitchen. The girl is very charming, and I give her the messages from her man amd tell her what he is doing in London. She listens, but makes me uneasy for my friend because she doesn't show much interest. We talk of other things, and of course about food. She tells me that there has been no bread in the shops for three days and when she went to the baker's that morning there was nearly a free fight for the available supply. She hadn't got any. I put down my cup for the last time and she lifts the tray to take it out. "Now may I give you a surprise, Mr. Brockway?" she says with a smile. "Certainly, if it's a pleasant one," I reply. She opens the door—and there is my London friend! Since I left England he has got a post as European representative for his old firm.

His Mother Taught Him Socialism

It is late, and the corporal has to take me to my Mess at Garath before he returns to his own billet. We lose our way, lose it hopelessly in the country lanes. It's midnight before we find the mansion of the coal-baron's mother, and the corporal has twenty miles to go. Wolf has a cold meal saved for me—the most wonderful salad I've had for years—and one of the German maids brings me tea. I eat and drink sitting in a comfortable chair in the lounge, whilst Wolf tells me of the visit he paid to Paefgen's home.

I have been greatly impressed by Paefgen. He is only twenty-one, tall and pale-faced, but he looks older and he has shown wide knowledge and adult sense. Wolf also has been surprised to find how much *au fait* he is with the British Labour Movement, despite the restricted sources of information. I'm puzzled how this young man, passing through adolescence during the Hitler years, came to be a Socialist at all. His home explains it. Wolf reports that his mother is a keen Socialist and secretly brought up her boy in the faith. His father, Wolf gathered, died at the hands of the Nazis, but he did not press his questions because he did not want to hurt the mother.

We climb the marble stairway to our beds. "Oh, by the way," Wolf remarks, irrelevantly, "Rolf got his girl-friend." "Does she work in the Food Department?" "No, she's a sales girl at a food shop."

THE ELEVENTH DAY

May 8th, 1946.

TO-DAY WE drive to Hanover for the all-Germany (minus the Russian zone) conference of the Social Democratic Party.* After we have been on the road five minutes I recollect that I want to speak to Tom Agar about the German "Bevin Boys." Rolf takes me to a police station and we are given priority for a 'phone call. This is one of the most prized privileges of the Occupation Forces in Germany. 'Phone calls are prompt—and free!

A half-pathetic, half-amusing incident at the police station. A small boy, stockingless and shoeless, enters. He is attractive and self-confident. "I've come for my bike," he says. "Your bike—where is it?" asks the police sergeant. "Here," says the boy, and explains. He lives in Cologne, lost his way yesterday and reported to the night staff at the police station when it became too late to get home. "Where did you sleep?" enquires the sergeant. "In the hospital," the boy replies. Wolf asks his age. "I'm nine," he says. As we set off in the car, we see the boy riding away on his bike, unconcerned as though his home were in the next street.

TWO YOUNG SOCIALISTS ON RELIEF WORK

At Wuppertal we have arranged to meet two young English friends attached to the Relief Service. We are early. Whilst waiting, Wolf chats with the German policeman at the door, noting the enquiries which a stream of men and women make of him. I talk with people standing about the pavement. One is a man who looks ill and old, but he assures me he is only forty-five. He has a stomach disease, and the doctors say he should have a special diet, but the necessary foods are unobtainable. Wolf joins me and reports that the enquiries at the Mil. Gov. door are all about first needs: rations, accommodation, hospital beds, certificates for vegetable seeds.

A Relief Service van drives up and the two young English

* Officially, the conference was for the British zone only, but delegates attended as "invited guests" from the American and French zones and from the non-Russian sectors of Berlin.

Socialists jump out. We go to a pub to talk. They are eager to hear of our adventures, but we learn some of the difficulties of their job, which is to find homes for refugee children from the East. They are working in a country district and meet with a good deal of obstruction, particularly from wealthier people. Then one of them makes an observation which sets Wolf and me laughing. "The Germans in our village were spreading a remarkable story last night," he remarks. "They were saying that the British are calling up Nazis for the army." Our friends can't understand our amusement. "How far is your village from Düsseldorf?" I ask. "Seventy miles." We tell them the story of the Labour Exchange notice. They laugh, but they also swear.*

A British Tommy Asks About Russia

We are on the autobahn again, crossing the Cotswold-like country. After two hours or so, we swing away to the right to the little town of Salzufflen, where Wolf's Berlin Nazi is in hiding—the Nazi who left behind a diary gloating over Jew shootings. Whilst Wolf investigates, I wander through the streets, enjoying the neat red cottages and their gardens of lilac. Outside the Forces' Club soldiers are waiting for a concert. I chat with two good-type youngsters about twenty. "Say," one of them remarks, noticing the badge on my arm, "you're a newspaper man. Perhaps you can tell us this—who are the enemy here, the Germans or the Russians?" "What makes you think the Russians are enemies?" I ask. "We've just been transferred from Bad Lauterberg, a mountain village on the line between the British and Russian zones. Six yards on the British side, armed sentries are marching up and down all the twenty-four hours. Six yards on the Russian side, armed sentries are marching up and down. Just as if the guns will go off any moment. What's the game?" "Perhaps it's to stop unauthorised refugees crossing the line." They both laugh. "You can't put that one over on us," they say. "We know what's what." They talk as though skirmishes had begun, reporting raids by Russian soldiers at night for minor loot. One of the boys tells of a raid where the loot was not so minor: two Russians got away with a lorry. "The British Commander sent a stiff note demanding the return of the lorry and the suitable

* A fortnight after I got back to London the press reported that the British headquarters in Berlin had published a *communique* denying German rumours that Nazis were being re-mobilised.

119

punishment of the offenders," he says. "The lorry was driven back across the line carrying the dead bodies of two Russians."

I pull him up. "Did you see it?" I ask. "Did you see the two bodies?" "No, but a friend of mine was on duty and he saw them." "I'm not accepting that," I say. "It's just a soldier's yarn." But as I saunter across the road I am worried. The disturbing thing is that British Tommies should be talking like this.

SHE IS IN CHARGE OF THE TOMMIES' LIBRARY

I see a shop window full of books. The sight is so unusual that I look at the inscription along the top: "Troops Study Centre". I go in. There are well-stocked bookshelves against the walls and standing on the floor-space, labelled "Fiction", "Drama", "English Literature", "Travel". There is an inner room with more bookshelves, labelled "Biography", "Economics", "Politics". I examine the books: they are mostly twenty years old, but many worth reading. I pick up some photographs, illustrating the work of the Centre—study circles, art classes, woodwork. At a table a young woman is sitting, reading a German book. "Who is in charge here?" I ask, wanting information. "I am," she replies. I enquire about the cultural activities. She is a middle-class young woman, well-dressed, speaking perfect English, the consciously clever type; she answers my questions with a strange mixture of audacity and cynicism. I pick up a photo of the Art School and ask her whether a row of pictures on the wall are works by the students. "Not at all." "What are they?" "British propaganda, I expect," she says in her challenging voice, her smile more cynical than ever.

At that moment a soldier comes in. He is from Norwich and recognises me. We chat about Socialism and the Labour Movement and the soldier exchanges a book and goes. I continue looking at the photos and ask the young woman another question. Her face has become hard and she answers with distant rigidity. Why the change? Is it my Socialism? Has her challenging cynicism been a reflection of a retained Nazi faith? It looks like that to me; but a Cultural Centre for British Troops is a curious place to come across it.

I go out and lean against a wall in the sun and watch the people. There are no signs of hunger here. Our car drives up and, as we make for the autobahn again, Wolf reports. He hasn't met his Nazi, but has confirmed that he lives here. What shall he do about it? After some debating, he decides to tell the story to the Political Section at Berlin when he returns there.*

WHERE THE ROCKET BOMBS WERE MADE

We approach a range of wooded hills. Wolf tells me that they are the Teutoburger Wald, the scene of the defeat of the Romans by Arminius (Hermann) in the first years of the first century, a place of legends and folklore. It is likely to remain a place of legends. Rolf points to a tower which stands above the rugged head of a range of hills. Underneath it, in the mountain-side, he says, were the vast chambers where the rocket-bombs were made. The workers lived inside the mountain, sleeping there, taking their meals in a large within-ground canteen, and having their cinema there as well as the workshops. Rolf adds that a few weeks ago the British blew the chambers to bits.

I want to relieve myself, so Rolf pulls up at an inn. In the yard a young mother is playing with a big-limbed boy of three. Wolf lifts him and throws him laughing into the air. "Well, that boy's not starving," I say. The mother turns on me. "No, he doesn't look like it," she says, "but he cries for food every night. He's so big that he's got twice the appetite of other boys. I have to give him half my ration." I think she is speaking the truth.

We enter the hilly district, the autobahn keeping almost level by bridging deep gorges. Little more than a year ago every one of the bridges was shattered by the retreating German army and we can see the huge white stone-work caught on ledges of rock or lying in the river far below. Serviceable one-track viaducts have been put up by the British engineers, each named after a famous battle of the war.

A CHANGE FROM LUXURY

We descend from the hills into Hanover and make for the Officers' Transit Camp where we had our meal on the night we left for Berlin. It has no beds available and we are referred to Mil. Gov. There we are referred to one of the Messes accommodating its officials, and at last find it, a villa in a suburb. We are shown into a large bare room with a single iron bedstead and a settee but no bed-clothes.

* He did so. British military immediately raided the Berlin house where the Nazi had lived and seized all his remaining papers. Whether the Nazi was arrested Wolf does not know.

After much scurrying round, sheets and blankets and pillows are borrowed from the rooms of two officers on leave. We sleep well, even if our beds are not as soft as those in the mansion of the coal-baron's mother.

"What are you grinning at?" I say to Rolf, who has helped us carry our bags from the car. "I was thinking of the soft beds at the mansion of the coal-baron's mother," he replies, his eyes twinkling.

THE TWELFTH DAY

May 9th, 1946.

THE MIL. GOV. Mess is reassuring after the luxury we have known at Hamburg, Berlin and Düsseldorf. The breakfast, served in a typical suburban front sitting-room, is good—still above home standards—and the lounge, where we carry our last cups of tea, is cosy; but they have not the flaunting plenty and soft ease we have previously experienced. The officers are mixed: some ex-army men, some civil servants, some technicians. They are a friendly bunch.

We call at the Mil. Gov. headquarters *en route* to the Social Democratic Conference to pick up a close I.L.P. associate and prominent Trade Unionist, Ewan Carr, who is in the Industrial Relations section: Ewan comes from Dundee and is the stocky, Scottish type. He introduces us to his colleague, Major Ashley Bramall* (young, classic-features under long silver hair), and to their German girl-secretary, Agnes Saager, who is an eager student of Socialism.† They are all coming along to the Conference and fill a second car. We drive through the centre of the city to the industrial borough of Linden, only half a mile away. It is badly blitzed, and it's strange to see long red drapings hanging down the fronts of ruined structures. The

---

* Bramall has since been elected Labour M.P. in a by-election at Bexley.

† Before leaving the office I got particulars of the Trades Unions and their memberships in the Hanover Region. They are mostly all-in Unions divided into industrial groups. Here are their names, with memberships as far as figures have been obtained.

BREMEN		
Metal Workers	.	10,465
Transport and Municipal		7,912
Chemical staffs	.	2,946
Building	.	1,807
Wood	.	1,735
Chemical and Pottery	.	1,458
Food	.	1,341
Technical staffs	.	1,110
Printing	.	479
Tobacco	.	244

HANOVER

General . . . 46,668
Railwaymen . . . 2,045

LÜNEBURG

General, Railway, Wood, Clothing and Textile, Building, Food and Drink, Metal, Public, Printing.

ALL-IN LOCAL UNIONS

There are all-in Unions in thirty-three towns. Incomplete returns give a membership of over 100,000 in twenty towns.

conference itself is being held on the top floor of an engineering factory which the R.A.F. somehow missed, missed but not by much. Nearby buildings are down and there are holes in the road and pavement right up to the doorway. But we see little of these holes—*they are covered by glistening silver birches*. As we mount the drab stone stairs to the fourth floor, we find silver birches on every landing and, when we enter the long, bright white-washed conference hall, dark green bushes line the walls and flowering plants are on every table. "How the Germans love flowers!" Ewan Carr exclaims.

The Conference Hall

Not only flowers, but colour. We had seen the red drapings on house fronts two streets away. The front of the factory itself is brilliant with red banners from roof to the ground floor, and across it runs a great streamer in white lettering: "*Freiheit und Frieden durch Socializmus*" (Freedom and Peace Through Socialism). In the hall the platform background is a rich red curtain and over it is another slogan stretching from wall to wall—"*Socializmus, die Gegenwartsaufgabe*" (Socialism Now!). But one's senses are influenced by something more pervading than red drapings and the bushes and the flowers: one is most conscious of the brightness of the hall, the long line of windows through which the light sweeps, the clean whiteness of the walls and ceilings. How can one help feeling cheerful and exalted?

A German comrade tells me that the workers at this factory have prepared this building for the conference voluntarily and from sheer enthusiasm. It looks in good repair now, but two months ago it was as dirty, and almost as damaged, as the buildings around. The workers repaired it and cleared away the rubble, they white-washed the walls, they went to the forests for the birches. How comes it that there are so many socialist enthusiasts at this factory? There are 4,000 men employed here. *Of these only sixty-five have ever been members of the Nazi Party!* My German friend says I have no reason to be surprised. Hanover, and particularly this borough, has a long socialist tradition. Linden returned a Socialist to the Prussian Diet in Bismarck's days, the only constituency outside Berlin (which returned six) to do so. I laughingly remark that Hanover is of historic interest also to England: our Kings came from here. "Not only came from here" the German Socialist retorts, "George I was buried here—until your R.A.F. shattered his tomb to bits."

I am seated at a table under the platform, or rather under the left platform, for there are two, one on either side, with a neat oak rostrum in the centre. We are a mixed lot at the tables—press men, Mil. Gov. officers, executive members of the Party. On the left platform are Social Democrats who have been exiled in other countries: I recognise Wilhelm Sander, who led the group of refugees in London during the war. The political section of Mil. Gov. has several observers, including Lancashire from Berlin and Luxton from Hamburg.

I turn to look at the delegates. They sit on either side of narrow tables which stretch the length of the hall: I estimate they number 600. There are perhaps forty women. Most encouraging is the large number of young delegates: quite a fourth are under thirty-five, and that means they were only twenty-two before the Hitler régime, graduates of the Red Falcons and the Socialist Youth Movement.* As I glance from face to face, it seems to me appropriate that this historic conference, the first for fifteen years, the scene of the rebirth of German Socialism after Nazi terror and war, should be held in a factory, symbol of the shattered conditions in which the restored Party begins (there is not a public hall standing in Hanover), symbol of making and rebuilding, symbol of the source from which its strength must come.

An orchestra takes its place on the right platform and the chairman comes to the rostrum. He begins a tribute to the comrades martyred by Nazism and the war, and we stand. It is a moving tribute and the silence holds us all. The speaking ends and music begins. We sit whilst the orchestra plays quiet, flowing music. There is nothing theatrical about all this. Everyone becomes a part of it, withdrawn to inner thoughts.

KURT SCHUMACHER'S SPEECH

The moment for which we are all waiting has arrived, the speech of Dr. Kurt Schumacher, the leader who has emerged for the tremendous post-war tasks of German Social Democracy. He stands at the oak rostrum—and I see in him all the tragedy of Germany. He lost his right arm in the first world war. His face has the pain of twelve years' concentration camp and bears its physical marks—his eyes are glazed and his teeth knocked from his mouth by Gestapo men. His nose looks abnormally large, because there is so little flesh on his bones. Furrows line his face. His lips are thin and straight. His shoulders are bent,

* The stewards at the conference are boys of fifteen—open white shirts, grey shorts, tennis socks. They are the beginning of the re-birth of the Red Falcons, the junior section of Germany's Socialist Youth.

his body is lean and he looks tubercular. If a film make-up man wanted to depict suffering he could not make it more vivid than in the person of Schumacher.

But what a transformation when he speaks! The vigour and dynamic of him, the challenge and strength, the humanity and the light of vision! And he can laugh, this martyred man. He has humour, sardonic sometimes, but at other times playful and friendly. Before he has been speaking three minutes one forgets his physical deformities. One is captured by his personality, one's mind is gripped by the concentration of his thought. He is no demagogue. This speech of 155 minutes is packed with reasoning.

It is not Schumacher's speech, however, which thrills me most. It is his political outlook. Here is the attitude which I have been seeking, a mind which looks to the present and future rather than the past; which attacks German Reaction and dictatorial "Communism" (with Russia behind it), but which also attacks the Military Government of the Western Allies and calls upon the German workers to engage in a self-reliant and independent struggle for Socialism; which denounces the dismantlement of German peace-serving industry and the dismemberment of her territory, but which at the same time strikes the note of European solidarity and world co-operation.

Everywhere in Germany I have found that "collaboration" has gone so far that in many minds the Social Democratic Party is identified with Britain almost as closely as the Communist Party with Russia. Schumacher has ended that now. As he speaks, I can see the independent Socialist movement in Germany being reborn. The 600 delegates shout their endorsement by cries of "*Bravo*", "*Richtig*", "*Sehr Gut*", their eyes shine with a new self-confidence, they lift their heads with a new-found boldness. This conference represents not only the organisational re-birth of German Socialism. It represents its spiritual re-birth.

I am intrigued by the way in which the Mil. Gov. representatives at my side react to Schumacher's challenging speech, which on some issues amounts almost to an ultimatum to the Occupying Forces. Believe it or not, they hear it gladly. When Schumacher makes the acid quip—"When the Allies buy a German to serve their interests, will they credit the amount against the reparations account?"—the Mil. Gov. men roar with laughter. This surely deserves to be recorded as a classic example of the toleration for which Britishers are famous! But there is more in it than toleration. I have found among the type of Mil. Gov. officers who are here, nearly all of them Socialists, a genuine passion for democracy, a genuine desire to see a democratic Germany come to life. They have been disappointed, as I have been disappointed, by the subservience of Social Democrats: democracy, the Robbie Burns philosophy "a man's a man for a' that", cannot come from that. Now the subservience has been given its death-knell—and even the representatives of the Occupation which has been denounced by Schumacher rejoice! I know this will not be the reaction of many attached to Mil. Gov., but I must pay tribute to its expression here: it is the most generous thing I have touched in Germany.

Schumacher himself is aware of the socialist sincerity of many Mil. Gov. officers, and his reference to it is really the corrective to what I have just written. "We admit that there are some good Mil. Gov. officials," he says, "but we cannot depend on the decency of particular officers. We must be independent and have the right to attack the Military Government. At present we have to function in a capacity subservient to the Occupying Powers. We want to be free. We want to answer for our policy not only to Germany, but to the world. Socialists who do not stand up to the Occupying Armies are not worthy to be members of our Party!"

I hope this speech will be published in full in England. I can only note features of it which impress me most. There is a refreshing break from the narrow Marxism and the rigid materialism of pre-Hitler Social Democracy. (I have always felt that the German Social Democrats recited Marxism most and practised it least!) Schumacher still holds to Marx and the class struggle, but he adds that Socialists can also base their convictions on philosophy and ethics. More specifically he says: "For us, Socialism is economics *and* moral values. The achievement of our economic conceptions is impossible without ethics." This view is also expressed in his attitude towards the Communist Party. He is prepared to collaborate with the Communists, as with others, on particular issues, but "we do not want lies, we do not want pressure from above, we do not want underground work in our Party. Where there is no democracy in the Party, there is no democracy at all."

Schumacher criticised the Mil. Gov. particularly for its retention of the "Himmler police" (I must ask about this) and the Nazi organisation of agriculture ("kept so that we shall have food, but instead of food has come hunger"), and for its

127

policy of dismantling the factories and shipyards. "We agree to the destruction of all war-potential industry," he says, "but we must be permitted to rebuild our peace-potential industry. We need to export to pay for our food. If we should come to the economic disaster of the 30's, remember it was that which led to Hitler." Most of all I like his treatment of the problem of security: "The victors are suffering from 'security disease'. In 1918 the result of this disease in the West was Hitler. What will happen now that the disease has broken out both in the West and the East?" He insists that the only security for peace is "Socialism of a democratic character in Germany and in Europe". Against the proposal to cut the Rhine from Germany he speaks out with finality: "It would end the last hope of democracy and Socialism. We should stop our work." He agrees to international economic control of the Ruhr, but Germany must participate in it and it must not be capitalist: "We do not want to exchange German capitalists for foreign capitalists."

THE GOVERNING CLASS OF THE GOVERNING RACE

Wolf and I take lunch at the Officers' Club with three Mil. Gov. officials.* It's a wonderful place—a lawn for sun-bathing, a glass-walled corridor lounge (like S.S. *Queen Mary*, first class), a large cocktail bar, and a restaurant which is almost a hall. The tables and chairs look new. Every inch of the walls is newly-painted, mostly in shining cream, and there is even a newly-done mural design in the restaurant of the British Houses of Parliament! The meal, generous and expertly cooked, is served by neatly-uniformed German waitresses. We are the governing class of the governing race, and everything tells us we are.

Except ourselves. The subject of conversation is Schumacher's speech, and in the sober review of this subsequent discussion the same appreciation is expressed as under the influence of his oratory. There is a feeling that he was too down on the police, which in most places has apparently been cleaned of Nazi elements, though there seems to be ground for criticism of some of its higher officials in Hanover.† Wolf contributes an interesting personal story of Schumacher, told

* Meals for delegates are organised well at the conference hall. Rolf is impressed by the fact that he is given tickets and gets the same meals as Dr. Schumacher. "Not like the old political bosses", he laughs.

† I took this up with John Hynd on my return to London, and he reported that the officials against whom complaint was made had been dismissed.

him by a girl worker. During the short period in 1944 when he was not in a concentration camp, Schumacher had worked at her factory. No one knew who the "little clerk" was and the girl, who had the duty of distributing papers and magazines among the employees, was puzzled by the orders she received from him, almost exclusively, for weekly and monthly journals dealing with economic problems which had nothing to do with his job. She regarded him as a "mystery man". The mystery is now solved.

I Deliver Fraternal Greetings

This afternoon I am to deliver a fraternal greeting to the conference from the I.L.P. Back at the hall, I ask for a corner in which to change from uniform into civvies. The men's lavatory is most used, so I am smuggled into the women's lavatory whilst one of the cloakroom attendants stands sentry outside. They regard it as a great joke. Fortunately the afternoon session begins with a ninety-minute report on the economic situation, which enables me to prepare my ten-minute speech. I am conscious of the importance of the occasion. Here is the first Socialist conference in Germany for fifteen years. I am the only fraternal spokesman from outside Germany. It is an historic conference and the circumstances make the greeting I have to voice one of historic significance.

I wish other Parties were represented. I wish the Labour Party were represented. There have been rumours during the morning that someone from the Labour Party will come.* It is pathetic how eagerly these German comrades hope it is true, how eagerly they applaud even *oblique* suggestions by Germans from London and Paris of goodwill towards them among Socialists in Britain and France. There are a number of Socialist journalists here, from other countries, Holland, Belgium, Denmark, Norway, but on the whole they are unwilling to hold out hands of fraternity yet. Wolf learns that some of the German Socialists from abroad objected to my speaking, but Schumacher brushed them impatiently aside.

My name is called. I stand at the oak rostrum with my Hamburg friend and interpreter, Heinz Heydorn. The applause for the first voice from abroad is ecstatic, followed by a deep hush of interest. As at Hamburg I begin with a passage in German and then pass to short paragraphs in English. I suggest there

* The Labour Party subsequently stated it intended to send a fraternal delegate, but no one proved available.

are three duties for democratic Socialists in Germany—first to stand for Socialism as the successor to Nazism, second to stand for libertarian Socialism, third to stand self-reliantly independent of the Occupying Powers. The speech has a tremendous reception, not because of me or of what I say, but because it breaks at last the isolation which German Socialists feel so keenly.* I cannot forget that the comrades in this hall were the first victims of Nazism, that they have gone through years of suffering for the Socialist cause which few of us in other countries have had to undergo. I am grateful for the opportunity to be the channel of the first expression of international solidarity with them.

The discussion goes on all the afternoon and evening. Three speeches interest me specially. The first is by my interpreter, Heinz Heydorn, who wins for himself a national reputation as the spokesman of the new Socialist Youth. The second is by the only woman speaker, who might have come from any branch of the Women's Co-op. Guild. She makes a much-applauded appeal to the Party to arouse German women to become political beings. The third is by my Berlin friend, Franz Neumann, who gets a great reception as a representative of free Socialism in the capital. Neumann tells me afterwards that the Berlin delegates have travelled in British planes. The Russians would not allow them to pass through their zone by road or rail.

The Left Among Social Democrats

I spend the evening in discussion with eleven members of two minority groups who were associated with the I.L.P. in pre-Hitler days: the Communist Opposition and the Socialist Workers' Party (S.A.P.). Nearly all these men had had long years in concentration camps and their faces, thin and lined, and especially their lips, turned down at the ends, show it. A majority of the C.O. have gone into the Communist Party, but many of them, including the host at the flat where we meet, have joined the Social Democrats, as have all the members of the S.A.P. I hear considerable criticism of the grovelling spirit in which the S.P.D. has operated in many areas, but there is general enthusiasm for Schumacher's speech and hope for the Party if it follows his line.

* The Sunday *Observer* reported that I claimed to represent "the British workers". No, I was careful to say that I represented the I.L.P. and "thousands of workers" outside it. That, happily, is true.

A Mil. Gov. officer, a reliable Socialist, and his German secretary, also a Socialist, are with us during this discussion. It is past midnight when we break up and a transport problem arises. The German secretary has a permit to travel by Mil. Gov. car, but not after midnight. How are we to get her home? An experienced underground worker, who says the habits of the police never change, advises us to wait until one o'clock, when the police are thinnest on the streets. One o'clock strikes and we set off. The underground worker appears to be right. The centre of the city is empty and we reach the street in which the girl lives without challenge. Then, at her very door, we see two policemen! We pull up and, their suspicions aroused, the police approach with their lights on us. One of them opens the door, turns his lamp from the girl to us. "I beg your pardon," he says, saluting. "I didn't know you were British officers. Good-night."

THE THIRTEENTH DAY

May 10th, 1946.

THE CONFERENCE is dull and I am glad when ten-thirty comes for I have an appointment with Dr. Kurt Schumacher. I've been reading his story in the *British Zone Review,* a monthly which has some good stuff and some appalling stuff. This character sketch of Kurt Schumacher is good, well-written and sympathetic. I guess from the initials attached to it that Noel Annan, a young member of the political section in Berlin, is the author.

A TALK WITH SCHUMACHER

One of the interesting things about Schumacher is that his new outlook and spirit defy his pre-Hitler career, which might have been expected to turn out a mind of the old official Social Democratic pattern. He was editor of the Party paper at Stuttgart, was a member of the Wurtemburg State Parliament, and was elected to the Reichstag in 1930. All the time at the core of the Party; how has he broken away from its rigidity and compromising nature? He must have done some thinking in his concentration camp! I meet him alone, except for Wolf to help interpret. Sometimes platform personalities are disappointing in individual contact; not so Schumacher, who leaves an impression of two intensities, which do not often mix —the first an intense emotion of earnestness, the second an intense concentration of reasoning. As I talk with him, I not only feel his emotion, I seem to *feel* his thinking. Another outstanding figure used to give me this latter impression: Philip Snowden.

Schumacher's dominant concern now, as shown in this talk, is to get the opportunity to make Germany Socialist, a good co-operator with the other peoples of Europe. He is confident in the re-birth of German Socialism: it will be better and bigger than ever before. Every day members are pouring into the Party,* and its leader is particularly pleased with the keen and

* Schumacher wrote to me in June that the membership of the Party in the three Western zones had reached half-a-million, all individually subscribing members.

able young folk who are coming in. He believes that democratic Socialism can win through in Germany—*if it has the chance*. The giving of that opportunity does not depend only upon Britain; but Schumacher feels that Britain, with its Labour Government, should naturally be the ally of Germany's democratic socialist forces and he longs for close co-operation with the British Socialist movement. Peace cannot be made secure by mutilating and imprisoning Germany, he says; peace can be secured only by creating from within Germany a nation which is based on fraternity among its own people and which desires to live in fraternity with all peoples. His last pleading word to me is to help to create the necessary co-operative spirit in the British Labour Movement.

Schumacher's personal talk with me is followed by a press conference with Socialist journalists. I have a date with two Mil. Gov. officials, but Wolf attends the conference and tells me about it. Some of the press men from neighbouring countries are not yet ready for international association with German Socialists. One of them impresses upon Schumacher that my speech does not represent socialist opinion abroad, not even socialist opinion in Britain. "I know that well," replies Schumacher a little sadly. "I know it and I understand it." Then he looks into the faces of the critics and challenges them. "But solidarity between us must come if Socialism is to come. Brockway, representing the I.L.P., is a forerunner. I am confident that before a year has gone the Labour Party will also extend its hand of solidarity to us. We are striving to create a Socialist Movement here which will be worthy of that solidarity."

A MIL. GOV. OFFICER HAS A SOCIALIST PLAN

The two Mil. Gov. officers and I go in search of a pub, the only place where one can talk. We find one in a side street, empty at this time in the morning. It is a proletarian pub, a bare place with an empty bar, windows still boarded-up from bomb damage, a few tables and chairs scattered about a carpetless floor. The hostess is obviously taken aback to see three Britishers in officers' uniform invade her premises, but becomes reassured as we sit and talk.

I am leaving Germany to-morrow from Hamburg, and before I go I am keen to get some ideas about what ought to be done here. I soon find I have the right man across the table. He is the clearest-minded on the subject I've met among the British.

His main criticism is that the British administration embodies no principle: it is inconsistent, muddled, topsy-turvy. For example, no one, he says, can argue that the control of the police or of agriculture or of Germany's economic life reflects the governmental power of Labour in Britain: they would be quite unchanged if the Tories were in power. He wants the Labour Government to declare openly that it would like to see a Socialist Germany and to mirror this desire in its approach to all German questions. Otherwise, he insists, German people will begin to believe there is only one Socialism possible—and that the Russian. "It is time our Labour people understood that British gradualism is not enough for the German crisis," he says. "The whole tempo must be changed. Already we have lost irrecoverable time. The Russians have lost no time: we have lost a year. Our indefiniteness is losing the battle for democratic Socialism in Germany and is handicapping the Social Democrats in their struggle against the Communists."

He instances his general case by the retention of Nazis in positions of economic influence. In many places the whole personnel in the economy down to the middle and lower levels are Nazis: very often acknowledged members of the Nazi Party until Hitler fell. He urges that we ought to think in terms of the time when our Occupation will cease: if that happened to-morrow we should have left the Nazis in power in industry and agriculture. Even when reactionaries are removed from places of influence, they are too often transferred to other places of influence.

I ask him how he would meet the objection that the Occupation Power has no right to impose Socialism on Germany. He says it is not a matter of imposing: it is a matter of allowing the Germans to do what they want. In Hanover, for example, the German District Commissioners asked that fire insurance should be nationalised—and permission was refused. He wants the election of the Provincial Parliaments speeded up and a public statement made that these Parliaments will be allowed to go ahead with schemes of national-isation and land reform. "The German people are not yet conscious of the fact that we have a *Labour* Government in Britain," he stresses, "a Government which stands for the end-ing of the old class relationships, a Government which would welcome their overthrow in Germany, too. Once the German people feel that, once they feel that they can count on our back-ing, they will be ready to seize the first opportunity to carry through their own social revolution." I hope he is right!

The other Mil. Gov. officer has been listening with interest and approval, and now he wants to say something on his own. His concern is the starved Trade Union press. There is only one Trade Union journal in the British zone, a monthly published in Hamburg, with paper so limited that the circulation is only 25,000. And the Trade Union membership in the British zone is 666,000! On the other hand there are three religious papers in Hanover, each with a circulation of 50,000. The political parties in the zone are given paper according to their membership, but no one seems to have thought of applying the same principle to the Trade Unions. The Unions are starved of paper even for their administrative needs. For the first two months of its existence, the General Union at Göttingen had no paper for membership forms.

This Mil. Gov. man raises a new and important point—the structural chaos of the new Trade Union Movement in Germany. The basis of organisation not only differs in the four zones: it differs within the zones (at least, within the Western zones). In some areas there are Industrial Unions, in some Craft Unions, in some General Unions, in some all-in Local Unions. Sometimes all four of these contradictory types are to be found in the same area. At my request, he gives me a broad outline of the British zone: *Hamburg*, all-in Unions with industrial groups. *North Rhine*, industrial. *Hanover*, industrial, craft, general and local. *Westphalia*, industrial. *Schleswig Holstein*, industrial with one Craft Union. This is not as bad as I feared. Hanover appears to have the most conflicting organisation.*

* I have already given Trade Union particulars for Hamburg, the North Rhine and Hanover. When I returned to London, Mr. John Hynd gave me particulars for the two other areas in the British zone: Westphalia and Schleswig-Holstein.

In *Westphalia* the following Unions are stationed at Minden:

Metal	5,978
Clothing	4,120
Transport	3,553
Public	2,879
Food and Drink	2,257
Wood	2,110
Building	1,611
Textile and Leather	1,552
Printing and Paper	1,156

There are also mining Unions at Beckum and Bochum, and metal workers' Unions at Bochum and Dortmund. Memberships are not available. (*Footnote continued on next page.*)

I hear the same praise of Walter Citrine and Ebby Edwards as I heard in Düsseldorf. Citrine shocked the "old Guard" in Mil. Gov. circles by referring to Hanover Trade Unionists as "our German comrades". Well done, Citrine! I also hear a repetition of the Düsseldorf criticism of another Trade Union delegation. I am told it did great damage.

RETURN JOURNEY TO HAMBURG

It is time for the Mil. Gov. officers to get back to their jobs—and for me to leave for Hamburg. They hurry off and I lose my way. When finally I get back to the Social Democratic Conference not only is the car waiting, but a group who have gathered to say farewell. They include Wolf (who is staying on a fortnight), Heinz Heydorn, other German comrades, Ewan Carr and other Mil. Gov. friends. As Rolf starts, I feel that something good has dropped away. Among these men, half Germans, half British, half Occupied, half the Occupation, are some of the best comrades I have known.

On the outskirts of Hanover, Rolf has to queue for petrol. We are held up at the side of some allotments. I get out of the car and chat with the gardeners. They repeat the complaints I have heard before that, whilst certificates for seeds can be got, the seeds themselves cannot be bought. Most of the allotments, about three times the size of English allotments, are thinly planted, but one I notice is rich with growing vegetables, fruits and flowers. I go over to it and note its contents: peas, potatoes, carrots, onions, lettuce, rhubarb, strawberries, goose-berries, raspberries, young apple and cherry trees, wallflowers, roses, iris. The gardener himself, a man about thirty of military bearing, is bumptious and self-important when I approach him. "I fought as an officer against France and Russia," he says. "I did not have the honour to fight against the British. I hope that we shall soon be fighting together against the Russians." He laughs as though we were already

In *Schleswig-Holstein* there are Unions at Kiel and Lübeck:

Kiel			Lübeck		
Metal	. . .	7,862	Food and Drink	. .	3,000
Railway	. . .	1,007	Railway	. .	2,000
Wood	. . .	677	Black-coated	. .	700
Agricultural	. .	614	Chemical, Leather, Stone and Earth	. .	500
			Dock	. .	387
			Cloth	. .	110

There are metal, building, printing and paper, and wood Unions at Lübeck, but the memberships are not available.

comrades in arms against Bolshevism—if I have met a Nazi in Germany, this typical ex-officer is certainly the man. Going back to the car I wonder what influence he has been able to exert to stock his allotment.

Food Calories and Moral Calories

We reach Hamburg and drive through its destroyed districts to the two lakes and the well-named avenue, *"Zur Schönen Aussicht"* (Beautiful View), where the Warcormess stands. The smiling German maid welcomes me and serves a meal, though it is late. Afterwards an officer belonging to the political section looks in to say goodbye, for to-morrow morning I leave early.

An English journalist in the bar asks whether Dr. Schumacher had said anything at Hanover about the food situation. "Yes," replies the officer (he had gone to Hanover to hear the speech), "yes—but only incidentally. He said that Germany needs moral calories even more than food calories." The journalist laughs. "How could anyone need anything more than food?" he exclaims. The political officer has his answer. "Have you ever starved?" he asks quietly. "No fear," says the journalist. "I've taken good care of that"—and to do him justice he looks as good as his word. "Well, I have," continues the officer in tones which hold our attention. "I was a prisoner of war and before the Red Cross parcels came, I was hungry all the time. Yet even when I was most hungry, I wanted something more than food. I wanted freedom. *That is what the Germans want.*"

No-one could say that without having reached down to fundamentals.

THE FOURTEENTH DAY

May 11th, 1946.

I AM up at 6.30 and have my last breakfast in the conservatory overlooking the garden. P.R.S. has ordered a car for me and I am disappointed to find that it arrives before Rolf and his car, because I want to say goodbye to the driver who has taken me one thousand miles about the British zone. A bus conveys us from the Air Office to the Airport and the plane rises with a happy company going home on leave. My mind is full of the crowded events of my fortnight and, the roar of the engines preventing conversation, I sit back in the reclining seat to try to sort out my impressions.

My main thought is that I have left a battleground. Yes, Germany is still a battleground. The guns are not firing, the bombs are not falling; but here conflicting forces are concentrated which will decide the future of Europe, perhaps the future of the world.

I think back to the Tommy in the little Westphalian town and his story of the armed guards on the "frontier" between the British and Russian zones. I recall conversations in Messes, where press men and officers have spoken as though a Third World War, with Russia as the enemy, is inevitable. I recollect the press conferences in Berlin with "high-ups" of the British administration: they did not hide their concern about the tension between Russia and the Western Allies. I remember the hope expressed by the Nazi on the allotment that Britain and Germany will soon be fighting together against Russia. If war *does* come, Germany will be its frontier—or, rather, the line which now divides the Western Zones and the Russian zone will be the frontier, with the three Western sectors in Berlin a beleaguered city surrounded by the Russians. In that event, there will be no hope for Germany. It will be obliterated in the atomic war.

This problem is a world problem, which will be decided in London, Paris, New York, Moscow rather than at Hamburg or Berlin. One would like to see Germany serving as a bridge between West and East, but at present under the Occupations, its own West and East are becoming identified with the power politics struggle of its masters. Germany might not serve as this bridge in any case (what a supreme historical atonement for Nazism and war it would be could it happen!) ; certainly it cannot do so whilst the forcible division of its people persists. One must hope that the Four Powers will resolve their problems before the Third World War is let loose—hope, and do all that is humanly possible to create the necessary conditions. A World Trade Union delegation is to go to Moscow, a Labour Party delegation of friendship is to go. Perhaps they may begin to break through the "iron wall" which separates the peoples of Russia from the West. Unless some contact between the peoples is made, there is little chance for the world and none for Germany at all.

I look out of the window and see the last of Germany, a green countryside crossed by grey-blue roads and dotted with red houses. None of those people below me want war any more than the people of Britain or America or Russia want it. How can their desires be made decisive?

I begin to think of Germany rather than the world. Yet the world is more than the background of the German scene. Under the Four Power Occupation, it is the *foreground*. Unless co-operation develops between the West and Russia, there can be no political and economic unity in Germany itself; there can be no pooling of its food resources (predominant in the Russian zone) ; there can be no psychological satisfaction of the German desire to be united as a people—and that frustration will breed a dangerous Nationalism again. Representatives of the Four Powers are to meet soon in Paris. If they begin to find a basis of agreement, there may be some hope that this forced disunity may end. If the division between them hardens, I can see the line separating the Russian and Western zones becoming a permanent frontier.*

My companion shouts to me that we are crossing the German–Dutch frontier.

I start thinking of Germany's frontiers. The cutting off of the territory to the east of the Oder, with its expulsion of population, has probably gone too far in hard and harsh fact to be reconsidered, but I fear its ultimate effects in history. The West has still to be decided. Of one thing my visit to Germany has convinced me beyond any doubt. If the Rhine is cut off all chance of democracy and Socialism in Germany for this generation goes. Even indomitable figures like Kurt Schu-

* The Paris Conference reached sufficient agreement on Italian and Danubian questions to justify the calling of the Peace Conference in July, but all the outstanding German problems remain unsettled.

macher say that. Fortunately there is little likelihood that this mutilation will take place. At present France alone demands it.

But no less serious than the territorial dismemberment of Germany is its economic dismantlement, and this is going on now. Let me get this issue clear. I met no democrat in Germany, certainly no Socialist or Trade Unionist, who is not favourable to the destruction of specifically war industries, but it is madness to extend this destruction to industries which can be of great service for peace, of value not only for Germany but for the whole of Europe. I don't know in detail what is occurring in the Russian zone, though it seems there has been vast dismantlement of factories and railways and that the only permitted restoration is of industries which can serve the Russian economy. But, under the Potsdam Agreement, dismantlement is also going on in the British and other Western zones—the destruction of the shipbuilding yards in Hamburg and of the steel mills in the Ruhr and the Rhine, for example. They were of course used by Hitler for building warships and guns and tanks and planes; but they *could* be used for peace, in building merchant and passenger ships and in manufacturing steel for industrial restoration and development in many European countries, as well as in Germany itself. Indeed, the coal and steel of Germany and the industries which use them are really the industrial core of the whole of Europe. Destroy them, and we not only strike a blow at Germany. We strike a blow at Europe.

We are crossing the Zuyder Zee. It is curious how the waves do not seem to move at this height. They are just straight lines.

How can Germany trade with Holland and her neighbouring countries unless she has industry to produce exports? She needs imports now urgently, particularly food. How can she pay for these unless her exporting industries are allowed to get going? She needs cotton and wool for her textile industries: stocks are getting so low that mills may have to close down—I heard that in Berlin. How can she export them unless her exporting industries function? People in Britain are not unnaturally complaining of the cost of supplying Germany with foodstuffs and other essentials. But how can the German people pay for them if they are not allowed to manufacture the goods which would meet the cost?

I mustn't get away from the real difficulty—the industries which could so easily become an instrument of rearmament if Germany again set itself to that purpose. They are centred in the Ruhr and the Rhine. The proposal is therefore being made that, even if the territory remain German, coal and steel should be internationalised. Well, here again, I found no opposition in principle from German Socialists and Trade Unionists; but everything will depend on how it is done. First, they ask that Germany shall be represented in the international control. That is reasonable and I don't suppose there will be any objection as soon as a democratic Germany gets functioning. Second, they ask that the industries shall be genuinely *internationalised*, that is, become the property not of foreign capitalists, but of peoples. They want joint ownership by the Governments of Europe; they would like European Trade Unionism represented; they demand that the productive elements in the industry shall be given a share of control through Workers' and Technicians' Councils. All of this is sound. If it were done, internationalisation would be a progressive step, a contribution towards the unification of Europe, towards the ultimate United Socialist States of Europe.

We are leaving land. The North Sea is rippled with white lines indicating wind, but at this height we are flying smoothly. The man at my side strains his voice to say that Belgium and Holland are away to the south, but, clear as visibility is, I can't see their coast lines.

Belgium and France. On the edge of the German frontier they also have their belt of coal and steel. Geologically they belong to the same coalfield; they also are a part of this industrial core of Europe. An idea! Why not link them up with German coal and steel and internationalise them all as one concern? That would be a serious beginning of a united Europe. The French and Belgian Governments could be given special representation on the Board. The French and Belgian workers and technicians could be given representatives on the administrative Councils. I believe this would do more to establish security on the western frontier of Germany than anything that could be proposed. I remember the film *Kamaradschaft*, in which we saw German and French mines separated only by an iron gate across one of the underground passages, the German miners going to the rescue of the French when there was an explosion. Why not remove that iron gate?

The R.A.F. boy behind leans forward and draws my attention to a ship far below. "A year ago it might have been a target," he shouts.

Hasn't this whole conception of security become nonsense with planes—and atom bombs? One doesn't get security by cutting off territory and destroying industries. That creates the psychology of *insecurity*. Even if a Germany persist of which other countries are suspicious, all the scientific authorities say that international inspection could prevent the secret manufacture of atomic bombs. And how could Germany go to war without them? But that is a negative resort: we ought to be thinking of the encouragement of a Germany of which we shall have no need to be suspicious. Is there the prospect of that? I think of the Socialist and Trade Union Movement I have found in Germany—that huge Trade Union demonstration in Hamburg, the metal workers and the miners of the Ruhr, the Social Democratic conference at Hanover and Kurt Schumacher. Can anyone doubt that the Germany they represent would become a good co-operator? What chance have they of becoming the decisive and controlling influence in Germany?

There is one element against them and one over which there is a question mark—the Catholics and their power in the countryside, and the disillusioned Nazi-taught youth. The Catholic Christian Democratic Union is an umbrella for the reactionaries, but part of its leadership and membership is not reactionary. Large elements of them can be won for progress if the Social Democrats take a less rigidly materialist line, and this they are tending to do. The Catholic workers are in the united Trade Union Movement, and this will influence them in the towns to resist reaction. The problem of the countryside will remain, but this is not only a German problem. And the youth? The Socialists have already won large numbers of them and, if they will be tolerant to those who were previously caught up in the Hitler Youth Movement, if they will infuse Socialism with idealism, they can sweep the younger generation, now mentally and spiritually a vacuum, into their ranks. After all, what alternative to Nazism except Socialism is there?

I pull myself up. I am shirking the issue of Russia and Communism. It is part of the world power politics struggle with which I began, and I can't find anything to add to my earlier rather unsatisfactory conclusions. Of one thing I am fairly sure. If the peoples of Germany were allowed a free choice, they would decide for democratic Socialism rather than totalitarian Communism. How often I heard in Germany the phrase, "We do not want another dictatorship!"

We have run into clouds and the plane is bumping—sudden drops which make one catch one's breath. A member of the crew says we are over England. I hope the clouds and the bumps are not of political significance!

I must hurry to apply these general considerations to British policy towards Germany. At present it is hopelessly confused: a mixture of the Potsdam view that security will come by dismemberment and of the socialist view that it will come by the establishment of a democratic and socialist Germany. It is time Potsdam was buried. It is time British policy was entirely directed to the encouragement of a Socialist Germany. How?

First, end the *military* government of Germany. I cannot advocate immediate unilateral withdrawal of our Occupation, because that would mean civil war, with Russia arming the Communists against the Social Democrats and with the re-actionaries awaiting their chance in the background. But why should the Occupation, whilst it has to last, be headed by the military with the political section subordinate to it? It should be the other way about: a political head and the military subordinate. The political head should be a Socialist—there are men in the political section who are fit for the job—he should have a Socialist chief for each department, and he should set out to animate the whole administration with the Socialist spirit. I have seen enough to know that it would mean a revolution. I think of that industry with a Socialist controller where every Nazi official has gone and German Trade Unionists and Socialist have been put in their places. I think of other industries which are still crowded with Nazi officials. I think of the British Big Business control of the Economic section, of the reactionary agricultural organisation which has been left, of the Socialist doctors shut out from the Public Health service, of Schumacher's complaint of the "Himmler police" at Hanover. All that could be ended by Socialist direction.

The plane is still bumpy, but the clouds are lifting. Is that Colchester below? Yes, I recognise the large red tower—is it a water-tower?

A socialist administration would not be enough. With some reluctance I reject the idea of immediately socialising every-thing. It could be done in Germany in present circumstances far more easily than in Britain, but, it would be a bad lesson in democracy for an Occupying Power to *impose* Socialism. On the other hand, we certainly ought not to be re-establishing Capitalism, allowing it the opportunity to dig in, and that is what we are doing on a large scale now. There are two immediate things which could be done. First, in the case of public services or key industries the three major political parties could be consulted—the Social Democratic, Christian Democratic and Communist. If they endorsed public ownership, there is no reason why it should not be put through. Second, if one or more of the Parties objected, the issue could be submitted to a referendum. This would be good education in democracy.

This line could be applied to-morrow: but we ought also to

be thinking of the time when the German people will be having their elections. At present the idea is to have local elections this autumn and provincial elections next year: I would bring the provincial elections forward. Suppose the Social Democrats get majorities—as they are expected to do in the British zone except in the countryside. Are they to begin from scratch, with no plans worked out for socialisation? Why shouldn't British experts, in conjunction with German economists, be elaborating thorough-going socialisation schemes in detail now, so that they will be ready for immediate application? That's a constructive project which would immediately give the German people the inspiring knowledge that large planning for her future was being done. More than on any other count, I met despair in Germany because it is felt there is no plan, no conception at all, of her future reconstruction.

This policy would make Britain stand for something in Germany as positively as Russia. We have a Labour Government with the declared object of establishing Socialism. Why should it not say from the housetops that it wants to see also a Socialist Germany? So long as the British Occupation persists (I would end it as soon as German democracy has got going and the Four Powers agree to "non-intervention"), why should it not be conducted in the socialist rather than the capitalist spirit? Why not, *why not?* If the Labour Government will do this; if it will courageously stand up to the indecent Tory clamour on the food issue and do more, not less, to rescue Germany from starvation; if it will renounce Potsdam and exert its influence to retain for Germany the industry which she *and* Europe needs—if British Labour will act thus, I have no doubt, from what I have seen, that a new Germany will arise cleansed from Nazism, moving speedily to Socialism, eager to co-operate with the peoples of Europe and the world for peace.

We are flying over the London docks, from this height appearing as mirrors ornamented with toy ships. We come to rows of houses, lined like a regiment, first dull grey, street after street of them, with no gardens; then large red houses with green gardens. The noise of the engine changes and the plane slants, the wing on my side dipping to the earth. We are descending on Croydon.

My thinking stops. Since I left this aerodrome fourteen days ago I have had the most crowded and moving hours of my life—moving, not only because of the suffering I have seen, but because of the renewal of contact with German Socialist comrades and the hope and inspiration their movement has given me. Never in such a short time have I learned so much and felt so much. But at this moment I must acknowledge I have only one desire. It is to get home.

To get home—and then to do what I can politically to help the creation of the conditions which will allow the new democratic socialist movement of Germany to triumph and, in co-operation with the peoples of Europe and Britain, to end for ever the fear that war will again break across its frontiers.

APPENDIX—LATER FACTS FROM GERMANY.

(Except where otherwise stated, the facts given here have been supplied by official British sources.)

New Ration Scales in British Zone.

The following scales were introduced on August 20, 1946:

	Calories per day.	
	Type I.	Type II.
Adults over 18 years	1,137	1,337
Moderately Heavy Workers . . .	1,338	1,538
Part-time Heavy Workers	1,509	1,709
Heavy Workers	1,884	2,090
Very Heavy Workers	2,445	2,645
Heavy Workers—Miners . . .	2,386	2,586
Very Heavy Workers—Miners . . .	3,477	3,677
Personnel working for Control Commission and the Services	1,537	1,537

Germans employed by the Control Commission or the Services also receive a midday meal or a card for 400 calories.

The official definition of Types I and II is: *Type I :* All consumers other than those falling within Type II. *Type II :* All non-self suppliers over 6 years (*i.e.*, excluding part and full self-suppliers) in all cities and towns, which, due to their size, bomb damage, or concentration in industrial areas, are in a particularly unfavourable position.

Author's Note : In broad effect, this means that the greater part of the population of most industrial towns (the actual number is 111) receive Type II rations, whilst the population in the countryside receive Type I rations.

Malnutrition Cases in British Zone and British Sector, Berlin.

(The Number of Cases of Hunger-Oedema admitted to Hospitals.)

Schleswig-Holstein :	July 31, 1946	97
	Aug. 16, 1946	177
Hamburg :	July	1,144
	August	1,206
Hanover :	No marked deterioration during July and August.	
Westphalia :	Slight increase up to July 31. No change in August.	
North Rhine :	No reports available.	
Berlin Sector :	July	163
	August	276

New Cases of Tuberculosis and Dysentery in British Zone and British Sector, Berlin.

Period.	Tuberculosis.		Dysentery.
	Lung.	Other.	
1945 July	1,984	254	1,868
August (5 weeks)	2,745	415	1,562
September . . .	2,597	298	583
October (5 weeks)	3,185	300	450
November . .	2,387	290	220
December . .	2,041	270	155
1946 January (5 weeks)	3,730	445	270
February . .	3,363	492	170
March . .	3,316	577	201
April . . .	3,373	596	224
May (5 weeks) . .	4,760	691	307

Nutrition and Health of School Children in Hamburg.
(Percentages of 8,000–10,000 School Children examined by German Doctors.)

Period.	Bad.	Medium.	Good.
1946 April (13th–30th) .	54·5	28·4	17·1
May . . .	32·6	61·1	6·3
June . . .	27·5	57·9	14·6

Earlier figures will be found on page 50.

Infantile Mortality in British Zone.
(Deaths of Children under 1 year per 1,000 Live Births.)

1938	January	.	61	1946	January .	.	136
	February	.	58		February	.	109
	March	.	54		March	.	109
	April	.	59		April	.	89
	May	.	64		May	.	82

Infantile Mortality in British Sector, Berlin.

	per 1,000 Live Births.			per 1,000 Live Births.
1938	58	1946 January .	.	150
1943	66	February	.	146
1944 . . .	120	March	.	130
1945 October . .	248	April	.	96
November . .	190	May	.	121
December . .	161	June	.	103

Mortality Rate in Hamburg.
(Figures Supplied by the German Board of Health.)

1938	12·2 per 1,000.
1945	16·6 ,,
1946 (half-year only) .	17·5 ,,

MALNUTRITION CASES IN HAMBURG HOSPITALS.
(Figures Supplied by the German Board of Health.)

In seventeen Hamburg hospitals, the number of occupied beds is 14,091. Of these, 1,020 are Hunger-Oedema cases *(August, 1946)*.

TUBERCULOSIS IN HAMBURG HOSPITALS.
(Figures Supplied by the German Board of Health.)

Deaths per 10,000 of the Population.

1938	6·2
1945	8·3
1946 (half-year only) . .	10·1

New Admissions of T.B. Cases.

1946	January . . .	499
	February . . .	567
	March . . .	1,017
	April . . .	1,121

EMPLOYMENT AND UNEMPLOYMENT IN BRITISH ZONE, JUNE 29, 1946.

Total of persons registered	11,865,100
No. of persons working for employers	6,300,998
No. of employers and persons working on their own account.	1,675,934
No. of unemployed capable and available for work . .	328,857
No. of unemployed incapable of work	391,210

Since February, 1946, all male persons between 14 and 65 years of age and all females between 15 and 50 are required to register; in addition, all persons employed and seeking work irrespective of age.

UNEMPLOYMENT IN BRITISH SECTOR, BERLIN, AUGUST, 1946.

Age.	Males.		Females.	
	Able-bodied.	Partly disabled.	Able-bodied.	Partly disabled.
14–18 years . .	459	68	1,080	105
Over 18 years . .	656	9,041	5,136	60,869

Author's Note.—The large figures of partly-disabled indicate the effects of the war among both combatants and civilians.

TRADE UNION MEMBERSHIP IN THE BRITISH ZONE, AUGUST, 1946.

Region.	Number of Unions.	Total Membership.
Hamburg	15	158,409
Hanover	79	266,904
North Rhine	29	410,350
Schleswig-Holstein . . .	47	47,336
Westphalia	39	271,022
Total . . .	209	1,154,021

Author's Note.—The *number* of Unions must not be accepted as an indication of Trade Union strength. They are, for example, more scientifically organised in the North Rhine than in Hanover, where many separate local Unions exist.

TRADE UNION MEMBERSHIP IN BERLIN.

In Berlin there are nineteen Industrial Unions federated in the *Freie Deutsche Gewerkschaftbund* (F.D.G.B.). They cover all four sectors. In August the total membership was 455,000, of whom 69,000 were in the British Sector.

TRADE UNION CO-ORDINATION IN BRITISH ZONE.

(*Author's Summary from Official Information.*)

A Trade Union Conference covering the whole of the British Zone was held at Bielefeld, from August 21 to 23, with the main object of setting up a united organisation under an elected Zonal Committee. Three hundred delegates were present from 200 Unions. The British T.U.C. was represented by Mr. George Gibson and the American Federation of Labour by Mr. Brauer and Mr. Kaltz, both former Germans.

The Conference decided in favour of Industrial Unions with occupational groups, but declared that the ideal form of organisation would be One Big Union with federated Industrial groups. Mil. Gov., the World Federation of Trade Unions, and the British T.U.C. recommended Industrial Unions.

STRENGTH OF POLITICAL PARTIES.

(*Branches in the British Zone and British Sector, Berlin, August,* 1946.)

Social Democratic Party	241
Christian Democratic Union	194
Communist Party	178
Free Democratic Party	68
Centre Party	54
Low German Union	42
Liberal Democratic Party	32
Socialist "Einheit" Party	31
"Right" Party	10
Rhine Peoples' Party	9
Democratic Union	7
Radical-Social Freedom Party	6
German Peoples' Party	1

There are no branches of the Socialist "Einheit" Party in the British Zone. The figures in the above table refer to the British Sector of Berlin only. In this Sector, Party Membership on July 31, 1946, was:

Socialist "Einheit" Party	11,021
Social Democratic Party	8,115
Christian Democratic Union	3,308
Liberal Democratic Party	2,193

Dr. Kurt Schumacher, leader of the Social Democratic Party, wrote to the author in August: "In the Western Zones we now have slightly more than half a million members. To them are to be added our Berlin comrades, who number 43,000. Our figures are *real* figures, and they are growing daily. The limit is not yet visible."